A LOAD OF BALLS

Alf Alderson

BALL; n. & v.
n. a solid or hollow sphere, esp. for use in a game.
The Concise Oxford Dictionary

Acknowledgements

A heartfelt thank you to everyone who helped me compile this book

© Alf Alderson
All rights reserved. 2009

Know The Score Books Limited
118 Alcester Road, Studley, Warwickshire, B80 7NT
Tel: 01527 454482   Fax: 01527 452183
info@knowthescorebooks.com
www.knowthescorebooks.com

A CIP catalogue record is available for this book from the British Library

ISBN: 978-1-84818-404-6

Printed and bound by Gutenberg Press Limited, Malta

A LOAD OF BALLS

CONTENTS

including Australian Rules Football

Bandy	Dodgeball
Floorball	Gaelic Football
Jorkyball	Knur and Spell
Korfball	Lacrosse
Marbles	Netball
Pelota	Polo
Real Tennis	Rounders
Sepak Takraw	Stoolball
Tchoukball	Torball
Water Polo	Zorbing

Introduction

Why is a rugby ball oval? How many panels are there on a football? What's the fastest speed a cricket ball has ever been bowled? And just why do golf balls have all those dimples?

These are questions that sports fans have pondered at one time or another, and questions that **A Load of Balls** answers, along with everything else you never knew you wanted to know about all ball sports.

Britain is a country of sports fanatics. Indeed, few countries in the world are as influenced by the motions of balls as the UK. If the England football team reaches the final rounds of a major international competition the streets become deserted during their matches, GDP rises and Tesco's profits soar; a British player makes good progress at Wimbledon and it's all over the front pages; and if our cricket team ever actually wins a major series then an open-top bus tour, a visit to No. 10 and decorations from the Queen are the very least the glorious victors can expect. So it's not something that happens too often, then . . .

But more importantly than that, balls invade our daily lives. We go out for a kick around, play beach cricket, chuck one around in the pool or have a knock up. We argue with friends and neighbours over ball sports, which offer a much-relished chance for the Celtic nations to get one over on the English, we gamble billions of pounds every year on their outcome and many of us define who we are by our allegiance to a ball of one shape or another.

Indeed, for Brits, football, rugby, cricket and many of the major ball sports are part of our national heritage – we may not be much good at them, but we did invent them all the same.

Yet few people know much if anything about the origins of the actual ball of their favourite sport, or how it came to be the shape and weight it is, or what it's made of, why and how.

Balls reveals all this and more about major sports and also ones you might not have heard of such as Snatchball, Korfball and Kittenball, explaining how each ball developed from, for example, a pig's bladder through to a high-tech lightweight sphere designed on computers and manufactured from space age materials. In each chapter you'll also find a whole host of weird and wacky facts, figures and quotes so you can amuse or annoy friends with that perfect argument starter: "Did you know . . .?"

For example . . . did *you* know that:

- 80 per cent of the world's footballs are made in Pakistan?
- The Marx Brothers' favourite game was Croquet?
- Two French kings died from Real Tennis-related injuries?

Well you do now.

If that's whetted your appetite then a browse through these pages will reveal a whole lot more useless, I mean fascinating, sphere-based information . . .

Alf Alderson
July 2009

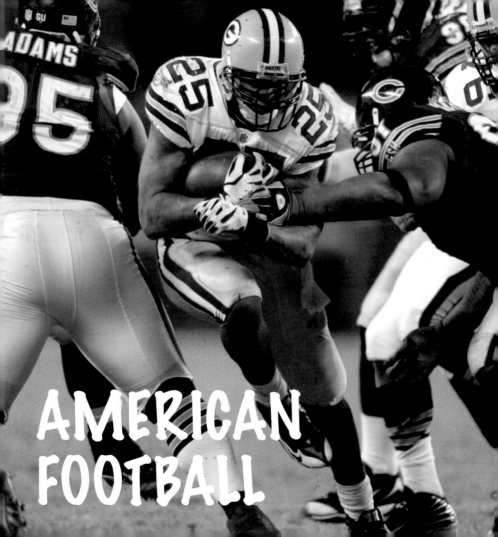

AMERICAN
FOOTBALL

ON THE BALL

"[American] Football is a game for trained apes."
Author Edward Abbey.

"Speed, strength, and the inability to register pain immediately."
Jacksonville Jaguars wide receiver Reggie Williams, when asked his greatest strengths as a football player.

"American football makes rugby look like a Tupperware party."
Sue Lawley proving that she's never played rugby (notice the body armour and inability to run non-stop for 80 minutes in American Football, Sue?).

CURVE BALLS

American Football today is considerably less harmful to health than in the sport's early years. In the 1905 season, 19 players were killed and 150 seriously injured, whilst three spectators died of boredom. (Sorry, I made up that last figure). President Theodore Roosevelt threatened to close the game down unless changes were made (they were) to make the game safer.

Apparently Hitler's rallying cry – 'Sieg Heil!' – was modelled on the techniques used by American football cheerleaders.

It takes about 3,000 cows to supply enough leather for a year's worth of footballs used by the NFL.

An American football is also called a 'pigskin' after the material from which early balls were made.

VITAL STATISTICS

Length: 11ins (28cm)

Circumference: 22ins (56cm)

Material: Leather for professional and collegiate games; rubber or plastic often used in recreational games.

Weight: 14-15oz (397-425g)

Pressure: 12.5-13.5psi

According to *nfl.com*: 'The home club shall have 36 balls for outdoor games and 24 for indoor games available for testing with a pressure gauge by the referee two hours prior to the start of the game. Twelve new footballs, sealed in a special box and shipped by the manufacturer, will be opened in the officials' locker room two hours prior to the start of the game. These balls are to be specially marked with the letter "K" and used exclusively for the kicking game.'

THE AMERICAN FOOTBALL

American Football's origins are not dissimilar to those of rugby and 'real' football (which to avoid confusion we shall refer to as 'soccer', in the American way). Early European settlers, mainly of British origin, are reported to have played 'ball games' in Jamestown, Virginia in the early 17th century that were not unlike the various mob football games practised in Britain. These had very few rules and used a ball made from an inflated pig's bladder.

By the early 19th century universities such as Harvard had very loosely organised intramural 'football' games (in Harvard's case known appropriately as 'Bloody Monday' and played between freshmen and sophomores). Princeton had 'Ballown' and Dartmouth had 'Old Division Football' from the 1830s until 1948, although this involved a round ball and in typical American fashion had one regular match which went under the grandiose name of 'New Hampshire v The World'. A five-team tournament called the World Series of Football was also played for a couple of seasons in the early 1900s.

The most notable feature of all these games was their violence – so much so that Yale and Harvard banned them for a time in the 1860s. Whilst we're on this subject, let's cut to the quick and ponder the interesting fact that similar games, like rugby, were never banned by lily-livered authorities in the UK, nor did they ever require kit that wouldn't look amiss on a Storm Trooper in order to participate in them.

The balls used in the above games were handmade in much the same fashion as rugby balls (see page 115), hence their essentially 'prolate spheroid' shape (the natural shape of an inflated pig's bladder). However, by 1855 manufactured balls were being produced with a more consistent shape which made both kicking and handling easier.

Two types of game evolved in the mid-19th century, the 'kicking' game and the 'running' or 'carrying' game, whilst a hybrid of the two known as the 'Boston Game' was developed by the Oneida Football Club, formed in 1862 and considered by some to be the first American Football club. All used the same type of ball, although consistent dimensions had not yet been decided upon. Shortly afterwards, the Ivy League universities were getting back into the sport with Princeton playing a game based on the rules of the English FA.

It was not until 1873 that representatives of Columbia, Princeton, Rutgers and Yale universities convened to standardise the rules for intercollegiate games, based loosely on 'soccer' rather than rugby. But by 1876 a further set of rules were drawn up based on those of Rugby Union, and the Intercollegiate Football Association was formed – so yes, American football is indeed a boring version of rugby.

As with most sports, rules have changed as the game has developed, the main ones being introduced in the 1880s by Walter Camp, the 'father of American football', which included the 'down-and-distance rules' and the establishment of the line of scrimmage, which saw the sport developing more definitively into what is now the distinct game of American Football, as opposed to being a variation of rugby and/or soccer.

However, it's the ball we're interested in, so we'll move on quickly at this point from the tedium of rules and regulations. Interestingly for such a technological nation and a strategy-obsessed sport, there has been relatively little innovation in the ball used in American Football over the decades – certainly nothing along the lines of the changes and developments of the 'soccer' ball over the last 150 years.

It wasn't until 1934, for example, that the circumference of the ball was reduced to its current size in order to make it easier to grip and throw. And brown-tanned cowhide – albeit with various forms of weatherproofing and a 'pebble grip' texture or tanning to provide a tacky grip – remains the material of choice for pro balls. The white stripes at either end of the ball are also designed to improve grip, particularly for throwing, and on top quality balls they'll be stitched on rather than painted.

Four panels are used to manufacture a ball, which is subject to quality control for weight and blemishes before, for premium balls, being hand-stitched together. An interior multi-layer lining is attached to each panel to provide better shape and durability, and all four panels are stitched together inside out. The ball is then turned

Rugby for girls, or a tremendously demanding physical sport? Sue Lawley and I differ on our opinions about Gridiron.

right way out and a three-ply polyurethane bladder is inserted and inflated, which provides better air retention and moisture control.

The last process is inserting the laces, which are noticeably more prominent than on a rugby or soccer ball in order to further assist holding and throwing. These may be made of leather or polyvinyl chloride. In the case of Wilson's 'pebbled composite leather' laces, they provide 'an astounding 174% more grip' than other traditional leather – not only astounding but mathematically incredible.

Other than improvements in the actual manufacturing process, the way an American football is made – and the resultant product – has changed relatively little for decades, and indeed the official supplier to the NFL since 1941 has been Wilson of Ada, Ohio, the world's biggest manufacturer of American footballs. They produce 700,000 a year, many by hand, with their Duke model being used in every NFL game for almost 70 years.

In a game that relies so heavily on modern technology and obsessive strategising, it's actually quite nice to know that the very essence of the sport – the ball – is one piece of equipment to retain so much tradition.

BASEBALL

ON THE BALL

"Well, boys, it's a round ball and a round bat and you got to hit the ball square."
Joe Schultz, Major League catcher, coach and manager.

"That's baseball, and it's my game . . . It's good for your lungs, gives you a lift, and nobody calls the cops."
Humphrey Bogart.

"England and America should scrap cricket and baseball and come up with a new game that they both can play. Like baseball, for example."
Robert Benchley, American Humourist.

"Baseball is very big with my people. It figures. It's the only way we can get to shake a bat at a white man without starting a riot."
Dick Gregory, African-American comedian.

CURVE BALLS

The average life span of a Major League baseball is a paltry 5 to 7 pitches.

A 'curveball' can curve up to 17.5 inches in the course of being pitched, travels at 70-80 mph and rotates at 1,900rpm.

John Smoltz, a pitcher for the Atlanta Braves, burned his chest while ironing a shirt that he was wearing.

All Major League baseball umpires must wear black underwear in case their pants split.

VITAL STATISTICS

Weight: Not less than 5, nor more than 5¼oz.

Circumference: Between 9 and 9¼ ins.

According to the website of Major League Baseball, www.mlb.com, the ball 'shall be a sphere formed by yarn wound around a small core of cork, rubber or similar material, covered with two stripes of white horsehide or cowhide, tightly stitched together'. Pity so few other sports are so definitive – it would certainly make my research a lot easier.

THE BASEBALL

Baseball, to the great chagrin of so many of its besotted American fans, originated in England. However much our transatlantic cousins may protest, its connections with rounders (see page 197) are blindingly obvious, and rounders is a game with medieval English origins. No greater an authority on the sport than pioneer journalist Henry Chadwick, elected to the Baseball Hall of Fame in 1938, claimed as much in an authoritative article he wrote in 1905 and – gadzooks! – although living most if his life in the USA, he was born in Exeter. Chadwick was also a keen cricket fan and instrumental in developing the obsession with statistics that is such a major part of Baseball, some

aspects, such as the box score, being derived directly from cricket.

Chadwick's claims were disputed by his friend Albert Spalding, baseball player and founder of the famous Spalding company, who claimed one Abner Doubleday 'invented' the game in 1839 in Cooperstown, New York. That has been placed in doubt by recently unearthed German documents dating back to the 1790s, which describe a game called 'English base-ball'. As Chadwick said of his friend, "He means well, but he don't know".

Spalding was also a major influence on early baseball, incidentally, publishing the first 'official' rules for the game which coincidentally stated that only Spalding baseballs could be used. He was inducted into the Baseball Hall of Fame the year after Chadwick.

But what of the actual ball? Before the 1870s baseballs were made by hand from a string-wrapped rubber core with a horsehide cover and varied enormously in size and weight – anywhere from golf balls to softballs in size and from three to six ounces in weight. They were renowned for their 'deadball' feel in play.

In 1872, however, the standards that are still in use today were established, and when the National League was founded in 1876 the Spalding Sporting Goods Company were granted exclusive rights to supply balls for league games. The balls were made up of a rubber core encased in layers of yarn and string and covered with horsehide, but despite – or perhaps because of – the standardisation of materials and dimensions baseballs still tended to feel 'dead' in use, hence this period, up until 1920, was known as the 'Deadball Era', with home runs a rarity.

That said, in 1910 George Reach of Reach Sporting Goods (which was actually acquired by Spalding in the late 1800s but retained the company name) discovered that using a cork centre produced a much more responsive ball, and such a ball was secretly used in the 1910 World Series (then, as today, the 'world' consisted for Americans of America and bits of Canada) with the result that the number of home runs increased. Thereafter cork balls became the standard for Major League Baseball.

After World War One the legendary Babe Ruth was able to make full use of the new ball to score unprecedented numbers of home runs – 54 in 1920 and 59 in 1921 (a record which stood for 70 years), whilst pitchers developed new styles of deliveries such as scuffballs to take full advantage of the more responsive ball. A 'scuffball' involved the pitcher making a smooth spot on the ball with sandpaper or some other rough surface, which in turn caused the ball to spin at the same time as travelling at very high speed. This practice is now banned due to the potential danger to the batter.

There were additional reasons for the improvement in the ball, including a move away from traditional hitting techniques in the light of Babe Ruth's success and the availability of greater numbers of white, unscuffed balls which were easier to see and thus easier to hit. On top of this, fans began to keep hold of foul balls as souvenirs, whereas previously they would hand them in for free admission to another game; and umpires would rub balls with special 'mud' that reduced shine and slickness without making the ball grubby, or would simply remove dirty, worn or scuffed balls from play much sooner – so much so that from the 1920s between 20 and 60 balls could be used in a game, as opposed to only three or four before.

The construction of the ball underwent another change in 1931, when a thin layer of rubber was wrapped around the cork core as the seams were raised. These changes

Toronto Blue Jays batter Aaron Hill takes his 'round bat' to the 'round ball' to 'squarely' score a two-run home run against Baltimore Orioles in May 2009.

had two effects – they deadened the ball slightly, and the raised seams allowed pitchers to get a better grip, allowing them to deliver more rotation to the ball.

It was over 40 years before any further noticeable change in the ball was made, when, in 1974, Spalding, still the world's major manufacturer of baseballs, along with Rawlings, changed from cowhide to horsehide covers for economic reasons.

Today, as with that other quintessential US sport American Football, Baseball still uses a ball that has changed relatively little from those of the sport's early days, which perhaps says a lot about keeping it simple and making it well.

Spalding's current premium quality ball, for example, the TF Pro, has a cork core, raised seams and a leather cover – not that far removed from the balls of a hundred years ago.

ON THE BALL

"Ball handling and dribbling are my strongest weaknesses."
David Thompson, Denver Nuggets and Seattle SuperSonics.

"The invention of Basketball was not an accident. It was developed to meet a need."
Inventor of the game, James Naismith.

"I'm tired of hearing about money, money, money, money, money. I just want to play the game, drink Pepsi, wear Reebok."
Shaquille O'Neal.

CURVE BALLS

According to a survey in 2007 there are approximately 300 million basketballs in the USA – around one for each person in the country.

A standard 29.5 inch basketball has about 4,118 'pebbles' on its outer surface to aid grip, with each pebble having a diameter of 2.5mm.

China's Sun Ming Ming is the world's tallest player at 7ft 8¾ ins. He grew to such prodigious height due to excess growth hormone caused by a brain tumour. However, this also made him very sluggish, but an operation to remove it cured the problem and he now plays for Maryland Nighthawks.

A Spalding ball about to be rebounded by Orlando Magic's Rashard Lewis.

VITAL STATISTICS

The criteria for a competion basketball are many and detailed and vary depending on the level, league, nationality and sex of the players.

The basic regulation sizes are:
Circumference and weight: (men) size 7 ball – 29.5ins, 22oz (women) size 6 ball – 28.5ins, 20oz.

The ball's surface is divided by recessed ribs of a contrasting colour to the main body of the ball – usually black on orange.

The International Basketball Federation (FIBA) also lays down a plethora of additional criteria, including:

– The ball must be free of toxic materials and materials which may cause allergic reactions, and must also be free of heavy metals and AZO colours.

– It must bounce at least 1,300mm when dropped from a height of 1,800mm on a hard surface with a mass of more than 1 tonne.

– It must pass a fatigue test where it is bounced 20,000 times at a reference pressure without leaking any air, and then perform to specification when dropped from the reference height (1,800mm).

– And a heat test where it is stored in a room for seven days at 70°C and shows no difference in appearance or performance.

THE BASKETBALL

Things ain't looking good for the traditional American sports – Basketball, being up there with apple pie and the Fourth of July in the 'All Things American' list, was, in fact, invented by a Canadian.

The man in question was one James Naismith (1861-1939) of Ontario, who whilst working as the chairman of the physical education department at the School for Christian Workers (now Springfield College) in Springfield, Massachusets was tasked with devising an indoor sport for the region's frigid winter months that relied as much on skill as strength and could be played in a relatively confined space.

Improbable as it may seem, he was apparently inspired by a childhood game from his native Canada called 'duck-on-a-rock' (although it's scarcely unique to Canada – children worldwide play versions of it) which involved trying to knock a 'duck' off the top of a big rock by throwing a smaller rock at it.

Quite how that led him to devise a relatively simple thirteen-rule game involving a soccer ball and two peach baskets for goals isn't readily obvious, but neverthless the canny Mr Naismith came up with 'Basketball' in December 1891. Thanks to the influence of his employers, the YMCA, the game was well on its way to spreading worldwide within two years of its invention – and by 1936 was an Olympic sport.

By 1893, the peach baskets had been superceded by iron hoops and hammock-style baskets, and later open-ended baskets were introduced to do away with the hassle of retrieving the ball every time a basket was scored.

As for the ball itself, from those early soccer balls (darn it, the English had a major influence in the development of basketball too . . .) it took only a couple of years before the first purpose-made basketballs were developed by the Spalding Sporting Goods Coompany (of Baseball fame) at the behest of Naismith. They were made from four panels of leather stitched together with a rubber bladder inside, with a cloth lining added to the leather for support and uniformity. Unlike modern balls they had lacing, but this was eventually done away with in 1937.

Leather remains one of the main materials of choice for the outer panels, although the moulded rubber composite basketball was introduced in 1942, which had the twin advantages of being cheaper to produce and less prone to wear and tear, especially when used on rougher outdoor surfaces.

The fact that basketballs may be used both indoors and outdoors is a major consideration in their manufacture. Balls are generally either designated for indoor use or all-surface use, with the former being made of leather or absorbant composites and the latter, known as 'indoor/outdoor' balls, being made of rubber or durable composites. Indoor balls are generally more expensive and may have to be 'broken in' first to scuff up the surface to produce better grip when in use.

It was not until 1970 that the NBA adopted an eight, rather than four, panel ball as its 'official' ball (still manufactured by Spalding), and in 1983 the company's full-grain leather ball became the NBA's new official ball.

The 1990s saw the introduction of new models of basketball with composite outer panels made from polyurethane materials, which allow a textured pebble surface to be moulded onto them. This pattern of projections and depressions provides better contact between the player's finger pads and the ball, allowing more accurate passing and shooting, and making it easier to impart spin to the ball.

An example of this is Spalding's microfiber composite 'ZK' model which became the official ball for the Women's NBA in 1997, whilst another major innovation was the company's 'Infusion' in 2001, which has a built-in pump. Then in 2005 came the slightly preposterously named 'Never Flat', which guaranteed that the ball would maintain a consistent bounce for at least a year.

Not all innovations have been well received, however. In January 2006 the NBA introduced yet another new official ball, Spalding's 'Cross Traxxion', which comprised two interlocking, cross-shaped panels with a microfiber composite structure with added moisture management to deal with all that sweat. The ball was supposed to offer better grip and feel, have no need of a 'break in' period and provide greater consistency between balls.

However, the top players were not impressed with the new ball, claiming that it was slippery, hard to hold and that the increased friction even caused cuts on their hands. Things went as far as some players bringing their grievances to the National Labor Relations Board. The physics department of the University of Texas was asked to test the new ball – and found that when dropped from a height of five feet the new ball bounced an average of four inches lower than the old ball, as well as absorbing moisture more slowly.

So it was that the Cross Traxxion lasted only one season before the NBA switched back to the old leather model. Kinda nice to know that 'traditional' is still best . . .

By now you're probably thinking that the only basketball manufacturer on the planet is Spalding . . . not so. Other major producers and innovators include Rawlings, which has produced basketballs since 1902 and is particularly known for its ten-panel 'RX10' ball – the extra panels aid with grip and handling; Wilson, whose premium ball is the 'Solution' which is designed to absorb moisture over the course of a game and thus retain its grip; and Molten, a Japanese company that provides the International Basketball Federation (FIBA) and the Olympic Games with a twelve panel top-of-the-line leather ball, the GL7. This design features a high-density cushioning foam below the surface, soft rubber seams, a flatter pebbled finish providing increased contact area and a flattened seam between the panels – the extra seams are said to improve handling.

Whichever the manufacturer, it's probably true to say that after the soccer ball, the basketball is the most ubiquitous sports ball on the planet.

BILLIARDS

ON THE BALL

"Whoever called snooker 'chess with balls' was rude, but right."
Author and TV presenter Clive James.

"A Thaum is the basic unit of magical strength. It has been universally established as the amount of magic needed to create one small white pigeon or three normal-sized billiard balls."
Author Terry Pratchett.

"For those viewers watching in black and white, the pink ball is just behind the green."
Legendary 'Pot Black' TV commentator Ted Lowe.

Billiards: Outer Mongolian style.

CURVE BALLS

Phenolic resin billiard balls produced by Belgian company Aramith require a minimum 5-tonne load to reach breaking point.

A cue ball accelerates from zero to 30mph in a fraction of a second when hit and can generate friction temperatures of up to 250°C between the ball and the table cloth.

Players in championship billiard games may walk up to three miles while circling the table and moving from table to chair.

Wikipedia lists almost fifty varieties of 'cue ball' games.

VITAL STATISTICS

Since there are at least 50 different varieties of cue ball games, for the sake of brevity we're only providing information on the most popular of these, namely billiards, snooker and pool (American and British).

Billiards: Played with three balls of 61.5mm (2½ins) diameter, no standard weight.

Snooker: Played with 22 balls of 52.5mm (2¼ins) diameter, within a tolerance of plus or minus 0.05mm (0.002ins). No standard weight, but all balls in a set must be the same weight within a tolerance of 3g.

American Pool ('eight ball'): Played with 17 balls of 57.15mm (2¼ins) diameter plus or minus 0.127mm (0.005ins). Cue balls on coin-operated pool machines are invariably either bigger (known as a 'grapefruit') or denser (known as a 'rock') in order to allow the return mechanism to differentiate it from the 'object' balls.

British Pool ('black ball'): Object balls generally have a diameter of 50.8mm (2ins), while cue balls (unlike American pool) are slightly smaller at 47.6mm.

THE BILLIARD BALL

English Billiards and Carom Billiards are the oldest popular forms of cue games, with roots from around the 15th century and origins that actually derive from croquet. Similar games can be found throughout the world – for instance the Asian game 'yotsudama', which literally means 'four balls', and the Finnish game 'kaisa', which uses fifteen numbered all-white balls.

Although English Billiards has been supplanted by both snooker and pool in popularity, Carom Billiards is still a very popular bar game in Belgium and the Netherlands as well as having professional players who are viewed in their home countries as pretty much the equivalent of the UK's pro snooker players.

Snooker replaced Billiards in popularity in the 19th century by which time the composition of the balls had moved on from their original materials of wood or clay (although the latter was still in use as late as the 20th century) to ivory.

Wooden balls were unreliable in terms of size, shape, weight and density for the obvious reason that wood is not a material that possesses any of these features in a consistent manner, and clay was little better. Ivory, whilst not being perfect (especially from an elephant's point of view), was a considerable improvement.

Ivory balls came into vogue in the 17th century, although they too were not perfect. They had a tendency to lose shape, absorb moisture and crack or split unless properly dried, so the ivory had to be seasoned for up to two years before being made into balls. In addition, the elephant tusks from which they were made would vary in density along their length and this led to inconsistencies in weight and mass even amongst balls made from the same tusk. It was only possible to make a maximum of eight balls from one elephant tusk since the tusk contains an internal hole from the nerve that runs the length of it, which obviously had to be avoided in manufacture. The best balls apparently came from the relatively small tusks of female elephants.

Worst of all, of course, was the impact this had on the world's elephant population – in order that fat-bellied gentleman around the world could entertain

INCONSISTENT

Consistency was a problem in early cue ball games, and not just as far as the balls were concerned. Slate table beds were not introduced until the mid-19th century, these providing a far better surface to play on than the wood used previously. Vulcanised rubber cushions were introduced shortly after. Prior to this, natural rubber had been used, but the bounce of the ball off it would vary depending on room temperature, and in cold weather the cushions had to be softened with hot water.

themselves with cue, ball, alcohol and cigars these gentle giants were massacred – by the start of the 20th century, up to 12,000 animals a year were killed to supply the British game alone. And this despite the fact that over 30 years earlier the exponents of billiards in the USA realised that making balls from ivory wasn't sustainable, long before there was any such thing as a green movement (other than that of the three-point ball in snooker).

In 1869, in response to a challenge from New York billiard table manufacturer Phelan & Collender to come up with an alternative material for billiard balls in return for a massive $10,000 prize, the inventor John Wesley Hyatt developed the cellulose nitrate billiard ball. Within a year this material had been patented (US Patent No. 50359 since you ask) and commercially branded as celluloid, the first industrial thermoplastic.

However, although it had the desirable properties of providing a consistent shape, size and density, celluloid offered one further property that was considerably less desirable – it is a volatile material and occasionally would explode . . .

This problem was eventually overcome by experimenting with other plastic compounds such as bakelite and crystalate, and by the late 1920s plastic composite balls became common, being used in the British Amateur Billiards Championships from 1926, and in the professional game from 1929.

Snooker gradually became as popular as billiards until, by the 1930s, it rivalled in popularity its less ballsy, as it were, rival. Snooker is thought to have derived from various table ball games played by British officers in India in the late 19th century, and indeed the name also has a similar origin.

Originally known as 'black pool', it was first played using fifteen red balls and one black, with the eventual addition of higher scoring yellow, green and pink balls, and then, later still, the blue and brown (although there is a version played around Bethesda in north Wales that uses even more colours, including orange). As for the name 'snooker', apparently this derived from the slang term for a first year officer at the Royal Military Academy in Woolwich – when a player failed to pocket a ball whilst playing with Col. Sir Neville Chamberlain of the Devonshire Regiment in India, Chamberlain supposedly exclaimed, "Why, you're a regular snooker!" and the name stuck in typically hilarious toff fashion.

Since WWII, snooker and then pool have considerably overshadowed billiards, with pool in particular, both American and British versions, having become enormously popular in the past 30 years thanks to the introduction of coin-operated machines into pubs.

Companies currently producing cue balls include the Belgian company Saluc, who make phenolic resin balls under the name Aramith; Frenzy Sports and the splendidly-monikored Elephant Balls, the latter two both producing polyester and acrylic balls.

Saluc is the premier name in cue ball manufacture, with 80 per cent of the world market. The company started making balls in the 1960s and now exports over 99 per cent of its production to more than 60 countries. It is the only company to manufacture phenolic resin balls, which have the advantages of being far more impact and scratch resistant than polyester balls and so last up to five times longer. They're also up to a hundred times finer-grained, which allows them to hold their glossy finish and leads to less wear and tear to both balls and table cloth. Production involves thirteen stages over a three-week period, which includes casting, curing, grinding and polishing before being hand-checked, then sent on their way to carom across tables around the world. And no elephants are killed at any point in the process . . .

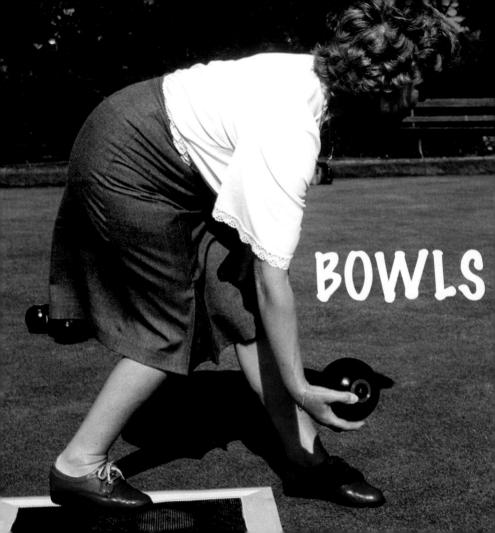

BOWLS

ON THE BALL

"There is plenty of time to win the game and thrash the Spaniards too."
Apocryphal quote from Sir Francis Drake, whilst playing bowls on Plymouth Hoe as the Spanish Armada sailed against Britain.

"I'd probably be playing lawn bowls."
Aussie Formula 1 racing driver Mark Webber on what he'd do if he didn't drive fast cars for a living.

"It has everything. Skill. Guile. Tactics. Uncertainty. Drama. Sledging even. And most importantly some of the best afternoon tea spreads on offer in Sydney."
Greg Growden, reporter on the Sydney Morning Herald, *sings the praises of lawn bowls.*

"If only Hitler and Mussolini could have a good game of bowls once a week at Geneva, I feel that Europe would not be as troubled as it is."
R.G. Briscow on fascist over-excitement in the 1930s.

CURVE BALLS

Between 1541 and 1845 working men in England were forbidden by law to play bowls on any day of the year other than Christmas Day – and then only in the home and presence of their 'masters'.

The 'crown' on a crown green bowling green is 9–15ins higher than the edge.

In a top level bowls tournament, competitors may play for up to four hours without a break, walk three to four miles and bend up and down over 100 times. And this is supposedly a game for pensioners?

VITAL STATISTICS

Jack
White or yellow sphere weighing approximately 225-285g and 63-64mm in diameter.

Bowls
Made of either lignum vitae wood, rubber or plastic resin and may have indentations to help with grip. Weighs a maximum of 1.59kgs.

Don't worry . . . plenty of time to finish the game before defeating those dashed Spaniards.

THE CROWN GREEN BOWLING BALL

The principle of bowls – using skill and judgement to bowl a larger ball as close as possible to a smaller one – is traceable as far back as the Stone Age. Evidence exists of men (maybe women too) 'bowling' rounded rocks at a 'peg', whilst it's also possible that the ancient Egyptians may have played a game that was a cross between bowls and skittles as long ago as 5000 BC.

In later millennia, the Romans may have played a version of the Italian game of Bocce, which is a variation of Bowls. There is also evidence that the Aztecs, ancient Chinese and Native Americans played similar games.

However, Lawn Bowls as we know it today is essentially yet another game with its true origins in medieval England, with records dating back to the 13th century of a game known as 'Jactus Lapidum' being played in London. This resembled modern bowls, although it's possible that round stones rather than bowls were used – and they may have been 'bowled' in a fashion more akin to putting the shot. In addition, a couple of 13th century manuscripts (one from the Royal Library in Windsor) contain illustrations of figures aiming both a cone-shaped object and bowls at a small jack. The oldest bowling green still in use is in Southampton and dates back to 1299.

Whatever popularity bowls may have had in medieval England was stamped upon by various monarchs at various times with various decrees outlawing the game as it was considered that it got in the way of archery practice. This was clearly of far greater importance for any English monarch worth his salt, who required a large, efficient force of archers to stuff the French. Indeed, it's in a decree of Henry VIII in 1511 that we see the first actual mention of the word 'bowls'.

Bowling was not forbidden to the gentry, of course, so you could play in your own garden or orchard (although you'd be fined 6 shillings 8 pence if you played outside it). Or if you owned lands with a 'yearly value' of more than £100 you could even get a licence to play on your own green – for £100. Not a game for the hard up then . . .

These bans were not applied with any real gusto by the authorities, however, and indeed it was in 1522 that the concept of 'bias', by which a bowl will swing to one side when bowled, was introduced into the game by Charles Brandon, the Duke of Suffolk, after one of his bowls broke in half.

The sport's most famous moment also came in the same century on 18 July 1588 when Sir Francis Drake supposedly completed his game of bowls on Plymouth Hoe before sailing off to despatch the dastardly Spanish Armada to Kingdom Come. It's almost certainly a myth, but how much more boring would both bowls and English history be without it?

The concept of the 'jack' was introduced in the 17th century, and this being Britain it could only be a matter of time before men with nothing better to do got together, formed a committee and invented RULES and LAWS. However since this is a book about balls and not bores we can skip the detail other than to point out that it all came about in 1848 in Glasgow, when clubs from across Britain gathered to formulate the laws of the game as befitted any worthwhile Victorian sport.

From this eventually came the formation of the Scottish Bowling Association in 1892 and the English Bowling Association in 1903 under the presidency of Dr W.G. Grace, better known, of course, for his cricketing exploits. The game soon spread around the world with most former colonies taking to it with enthusiasm, although the world headquarters have remained in Edinburgh.

As regards the technical composition of bowls, for centuries they were rather crude spherical objects made from dense, heavy wood (hence the terms 'woods' to describe them) known as 'lignum vitae', or even of cast iron. Wooden bowls would be shaped by hand and thus didn't have a consistent shape and weight, but during the latter years of the 19th century various innovations resulted in more consistency in their manufacture.

Amongst these was the development by Scottish company Thomas Taylor (still very much in business today, incidentally) of a machine for shaping bowls with consistent shape and size along with the world's first testing table for bias of bowls.

IT'S ALL A LOAD OF BALLS – A few Bowls terms

BURNED END
A 'burned end' is one where the jack has been moved outside the boundaries of the rink by a bowl in play. In normal competition burned ends must be replayed.

DRAW
A 'dead draw' is an attempt to deliver the bowl as close as possible to the target (generally the jack).

DRIVE
A shot where the player delivers the bowl with maximum force toward the target. Known in Scotland as a 'blooter'.

GUARD
A bowl played such that it restricts the opposition from getting to the target.

JACK
You should know what this is by now, but it's also referred to colloquially as the 'white', the 'kitty' or the 'sweetie'.

LINE OR ROAD
The 'line' or 'road' is the curved route taken to the jack as a result of bias.

WEIGHT
Term used to refer to the power applied to a delivery.

Another major influence on the technical development of bowls came from the American company Henselite, which introduced the world's first one piece moulded and machined composite plastic bowls in the 1930s, followed by a variety of innovations after the war, including the introduction of dimples for better grip. The company's Henselite Classic bowl is now the world's most popular bowl outside Australia and New Zealand where consistently faster greens dictate the use of 'narrow biased' models.

Which brings us nicely – and very briefly – on to 'bias'. The concept of a ball that is made to deliberately veer off course is perhaps unique to bowls since most other ball manufacturers aim for unerring accuracy from their products when in use, but a bowl's bias is nevertheless meant to be consistent. Bias was originally produced by inserting weights into one side of the bowl, but now is produced as a result of the shape of the bowl.

Modern bowls are available in a variety of colours and a 'set' (bowls come in sets of four) will have unique symbols engraved on them for identification. One side of the bowl will have a large symbol within a circle – this indicates the side away from the bias – whilst the other side will have a small symbol within a circle to indicate the bias side, or the side towards which the bowl will turn when bowled.

Bowling has developed into several different formats, including lawn bowls, crown green bowls, short mat bowls (played on a 'mat' of 12.2 to 13.7m in length), indoor bowls, carpet bowls (played on a moveable carpet of 9.1 x 1.82m) and federation bowls, all of which retain the essential element of aiming your bowl as close as possible to the jack.

CRICKET

ON THE BALL

"Cricket civilizes people and creates good gentlemen."
Robert Mugabe, I kid you not . . .

"I have always looked on cricket as organised loafing."
William Temple (1881-1944), Archbishop of Canterbury.

"An act of cowardice and I consider it appropriate that the
Australian team were wearing yellow."
*New Zealand Prime Minister Rob Muldoon, after Australian
bowler Trevor Chappell bowled underarm for the final delivery in
a 1981 test between New Zealand and Australia to prevent the
Kiwis scoring the six they required to tie the match.*

CURVE BALLS

Frederick, Prince of Wales (1707 – 1751) is said to have died from an abscess caused as a result of being hit on the head by a cricket ball. The story is apocryphal, but it sounds good, as does his epigram, penned by William Makepeace Thackeray – 'Here lies poor Fred, who was alive and is now dead.'

In August 1947 during a club match in Manchester a Miss Stone was hit by a ball whacked out of the ground by an enthusiastic batsman. She sued for her injury, claiming that the ball was not only a nuisance but a dangerous item that had 'escaped' from the ground. The judge, Lord Normand, threw the case out with the perspicacious comment, "It is not the law that precautions must be taken against every peril that can be foreseen by the timorous."

The first man recorded as actually being killed by a cricket ball was the unfortunate George Summers, who was done in by a ball which struck him in the head after ricocheting off a stone during a game between Nottinghamshire and MCC in 1871.

VITAL STATISTICS

Weight: 5.5–5.75oz (155.9–163g).

Circumference: 8¾ins–9ins (224–229mm).

Balls used in women's and youth matches are slightly smaller (e.g. women's balls weigh 5oz (140g); youth (or colt) balls weight 4¾oz (133g).

White balls swing more than red balls – fact. As proved on *Tomorrow's World*.

TYPES OF CRICKET BALL DELIVERY

Full toss/Beamer	Bouncer	Indipper	Inswinger
Leg cutter	Yorker	Off cutter	Outdipper
Reverse	Slower Ball	Outswinger	Arm ball
Doosra	Flipper	Googly	Leg break
Off break	Slider	Topspinner	

CLASSIFICATION OF PACE BOWLERS

	mph	kmph
Fast (Express)	90+	145+
Fast-Medium	80 - 89	129 - 145
Medium-Fast	70 - 79	113 - 129
Medium	60 - 69	97 - 113
Medium-Slow	50 - 59	80 - 97
Slow-Medium	40 - 49	64 - 80
Slow	below 40	below 64

Shoaib Akhtar of Pakistan and Brett Lee of Australia are considered the fastest bowlers in history – both have topped 100mph.

The world's first – and probably only – diamond cricket ball was made in Sri Lanka in 2004. It was encrusted with 2,704 diamonds and had 18 carat gold stitching on the seam. Material similar to that used on the wings of NASA Space Shuttles secured the diamonds, presumably ensuring they stay in place when the ball is whacked for six . . .

THE CRICKET BALL

Over time cricket balls have been made from materials as varied as a sheep's wool/sheep shit combo to diamonds; they have been the main protagonist in court cases; they have rubbed vigorously against a million groins; and they have been the source of endless discussions over warm pints and cold lagers.

Despite all this, the essential ingredients of what is possibly the most debated sphere in the sporting world are a core of cork layered with tightly wound string, which is then covered by a leather case. The case is made from four separate pieces of leather with one half rotated at 90 degrees to the other, and a raised seam between these two halves which is sewn together with six rows of stitches made from string – the other two pieces of leather are left unstitched. The ball will then usually be dyed red, although other colours such as orange and yellow have been used for improved visibility, along with white for floodlit matches.

Things were not always so high tech. Early cricket balls were as basic as it comes – a lump of wood was used in an 8th century Punjab bat-and-ball game called Gilli-danda, which some believe to be an ancestor of cricket; and medieval records indicate that something akin to cricket was being played in the Weald area of south east England shortly after the Norman invasion of 1066, which involved throwing stones or dingleberries at a no-doubt desperate opponent using a tree trunk or gate as a wicket.

Other early written references to cricket also refer to the sport being played in south east England in the late 16th and early 17th centuries, in particular a record from 1611 shows two men in Sussex being fined for playing cricket on a Sunday instead of going to church, although with only two players it really can't have been much of a game.

It's thought that 17th century cricketers played the game with balls made from leather, stuffed with cloth, hair and feathers, or a mix of cork and wool known as a 'quilt', although no hard proof exists for any of this. There is, however, evidence that the balls were hard, whatever they were made from. A 1658 poem, 'The Mysteries of

Love' by Edward Phillips remarks coyly, 'Would my eyes had been beat out of my head with a cricket ball the day before I saw thee'. Hmm . . .

By the early 18th century cricket was well established as the sport of 'gentlemen'. The hoi polloi were hired to bowl gentle underarm lobs to said gentlemen, who could then whack the ball into the skies. Organised inter-county and university games ensued, whilst in 1744 the first version of the Laws of Cricket was drawn up.

The first official regulations for the ball's maximum weight appeared in 1774, around the same time as underarm bowling began to be replaced by faster, more challenging and potentially lethal overarm bowling. Bowlers realised that overarm bowling enabled them to pitch the ball at different lengths and varying speeds, which gave them more chance of getting the batsman out, and the introduction of a regulation size and weight for the ball helped further, since it made the delivery slightly more predictable.

The estimably-named Edward 'Lumpy' Stevens of Chertsey and Surrey was one of the first bowlers to use the overarm pitched delivery effectively, and like modern bowlers he would experiment with speed, length and line of delivery.

To supply this burgeoning sporting development the Duke family from the Eden Valley in Kent had set up a cottage industry in 1760 manufacturing the first six-seamed cricket ball, an obvious forerunner of those used today. The Dukes owed their success to employing 'quiltwinders' (as cricket ball makers were known) who had the arcane skills to be able to wind a length of thread around an octagonal piece of cork to make an effective core for the leather-bound ball.

There was a practical reason behind this use of a cork core – it gave bounce and hardness to the ball at the same time as providing enough 'give' to ensure that the wooden cricket bats were not damaged. The stitching around the ball also had to be squashed down to create a reasonably spherical shape. This was done with an instrument called, not surprisingly, a 'squeezer'. More surprising is the fact that squeezers were often constructed from railway sleeper bolts, which were purloined by workers who walked to the factory along the railway track from nearby Tonbridge. The

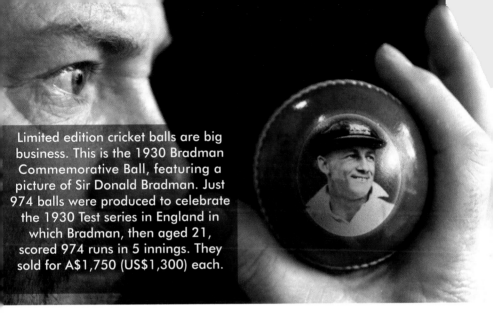

Limited edition cricket balls are big business. This is the 1930 Bradman Commemorative Ball, featuring a picture of Sir Donald Bradman. Just 974 balls were produced to celebrate the 1930 Test series in England in which Bradman, then aged 21, scored 974 runs in 5 innings. They sold for A$1,750 (US$1,300) each.

quality of Duke cricket balls was such that in 1852 their triple seam ball won a prize medal at the Great Exhibition in London. Duke cricket balls are still in production today, although they haven't been manufactured in the Eden Valley since 1994 – indeed, they are said to keep their shine longer than other balls (whilst Indian-made balls supposedly wear better and Aussie Kookaburra balls have a more raised seam to give additional purchase).

Kookaburra, one of the world's major manufacturers of cricket balls, provides all the balls for one day internationals and 85 per cent of those used in Test cricket. The company was established in the late 19th century by English émigré Alfred Grace Thompson. Like all other successful cricket ball manufacturers they moved from labour intensive hand-sewn balls to machine manufactured products, opening a custom built

FINGER PICKING GOOD

By picking at and tampering with the ball it's possible to affect the way it pitches and swings since the condition of a ball's outer surface will affect the way it moves through the air. 'Ball tampering' remains a controversial feature of cricket to this day. The rules of the game state that it's forbidden to:

* rub any substance apart from saliva or sweat onto the ball
* rub the ball on the ground
* scuff the ball with any rough object, including the fingernails
* pick at or lift the seam of the ball

But as in any professional sport it takes more than mere rules to oblige some sportsmen and women to play according to the rules.

Umpires will inspect the ball regularly during a match, and some 'tampering' is allowed – a player may polish the ball as long as no artificial substance is used (hence the frantic pumping of the ball against the inner groin by bowlers and fielders between deliveries to polish one side of the ball so it 'swings' in the air). Wet balls can be dried on a towel; and mud or dirt may be removed under the umpire's supervision; but any interference with the seam or roughening of the surface is strictly illegal and has on numerous occasions caused a brouhaha in Test, County and minor league cricket.

---

plant in Melbourne in 1946 and later developing state-of-the-art machines for cricket ball manufacture.

A similar path was followed in the UK by Alfred Reader & Co. Reader, from Kent, was a grocer and postmaster before moving into the manufacture of cricket balls in the late 19th century. His company became one of the largest manufacturers of cricket balls in the UK, and by the 1970s was using high-tech research and development to produce balls made from synthetic cork in partnership with the Tiflex company from Liskeard in Cornwall. The company specialises in research into impact abrasion and vibration-absorbing compounds using multi-million pound R&D equipment – ideally suited to cricket ball development then.

Tiflex's top-of-the-range ball is the 'Oxbridge ECB', designed for first-class and international cricket and made from a high-tech bonded cork and rubber core encased in alum-tanned English leather with a wax finish – a snip at £60 each, and a far cry from a lump of sheep dung, wool and grass flying across a grassy heath.

As for the traditional deep red colour of cricket balls, again reasons for this seem lost in the mist of time. One postulation is that it may have derived from reddle or ochre which was used to brand sheep, although my own thoughts are that it's useful for masking the blood of injured batsmen.

One-day matches played under floodlights saw the introduction of white balls which are more visible to both players and spectators. However, this is cricket we're talking about which inevitably means that such innovation was controversial. Players reported that white balls would swing more and deteriorate faster than red balls. There were also claims that the ball was harder, hurt fielders' hands and could even break bats.

The polyurethane coating added to a white ball to prevent it getting dirty was the reason for the extra swing, and this was proved under the rigorously testing conditions of the BBC's *Tomorrow's World* studio in 1999 when Dr. Brian Wilkins of New Zealand demonstrated with his homemade bowling machine that white balls swing more than red, at the same time reassuringly confirming what an utterly idiosyncratic sport cricket is.

BOWLED OVER – TYPES OF BOWLER

Swing bowlers use the seam of the ball to make it travel in a curved path through the air. They will polish one side of the ball whilst allowing the other to become rough and worn as this helps to increase the amount of swing. For the technically-minded, swing occurs as a result of differing airflows between the smooth and rough side of the ball.

On top of this the bowler can vary the ball's swing into or away from the batsman depending on the way he holds it when bowling. And just to make things even more tricky for the poor old batsman, the swing of a ball is also affected by damp or humid weather conditions.

Spin bowlers, as the name suggests, make the ball spin in order to fox the batsman. There are two broad categories of spin bowling: wrist spin and finger spin, which use the eponymous parts of the anatomy to impart spin. Speed is far less important for spin bowlers than swing bowlers, hence their leisurely amble to the crease when making a delivery.

Slow bowlers are an increasingly rare species who bowl at the same speed as spinners, but don't actually spin the ball. So what's the point?, you might think. Precisely. That's why they're dying out, although those with great accuracy in line and length and a good variety of speeds (albeit slow speeds) are still valued.

Because a ball's characteristics change during a game, fast bowlers will prefer to play with a new ball since it'll be harder, travel faster and bounce more, whereas older balls are better for spin bowlers as their rougher surface imparts better spin. In Test matches a new ball is used from the start of each innings and a new one offered to the fielding captain to take every 80 overs.

CROQUET

ON THE BALL

"Croquet is tough. People play for months because the rules are so bizarre. Those crazy English."
US actress Jane Kaczmarek.

"Your Majesty, members of the jury, loyal subjects . . . and the King . . . the prisoner at the bar stands accused of enticing Her Majesty, the Queen of Hearts, into a game of croquet, thereby causing the Queen to lose her temper."
The White Rabbit puts Alice on trial in Alice in Wonderland.

"Among US croquet players: Publisher William Randolph Hearst . . . and the four Marx Brothers. Most of these play according to the Wimbledon Championship rules and all of them take the game as seriously as Britons their cricket."
Time *magazine on croquet, 3 July 1939.*

CURVE BALLS

Croquet balls come in three 'sets' of colours:
First set – blue, red, black, yellow.
Second set – brown, white, green, pink.
Third set – aubergine, peach, slate, porridge (nice!).
And the Americans have a fourth, additional, format of their own – striped primary colours with a white 1.25 inch band around the ball.

On a hot English summer day (yes, they do occur from time to time) the surface temperature of a black croquet ball has been measured at 66.2°C (151.2°F) compared to 48.4°C (119.1°F) for a yellow ball. (Dr. I. Plummer, 2005).

During WWII, British croquet ball manufacturer Jaques also produced board games to be sent out to British POWs in Nazi Germany. Built into them were secret compartments which held hacksaws, maps and currency to assist with escape attempts.

VITAL STATISTICS

Diameter: 92mm, +/- 0.8mm (3½ins +/- 1/32 in).

Weight: 454g, +/- 7g (16oz, +/- ¼ oz).

Material: Composite plastic.

Milling: The pattern must consist of two orthogonal sets of grooves and the width of the grooves must be less than the width of the upstands left after grooving.

Balls used for recreational play may be lighter and may lack any surface milling.

THE CROQUET BALL

Improbable as it may seem bearing in mind the genteel image that is nowadays associated with croquet, this was once the bad boy of the sporting world. Croquet was banned in some sports clubs and denounced by some members of the clergy, mainly on the basis that it was popular with women (much the same as some golf clubs these days). That, of course, would never do.

The game's early origins are a little obscure. There's plenty of evidence of mallet and ball games from medieval Britain and Europe which involved knocking a single crude wooden ball through a willow hoop (unlike croquet which uses more than one ball), one of which was called 'closh', but the definitions and rules of these games are hazy.

Better known is forerunner 'pall mall', a slightly later game which originated in France where it was called *paille maille*, the name referring to the mallet rather than the actual game. References to 'pall mall' in England date back to 1568, while Samuel Pepys comments on the game in his diaries of 1661. It involved whacking a ball along a pitch up to 1,000 metres long and ended when said ball was scooped into a raised hoop.

The game Pepys referred to was being played by the Duke of York near St. James's Palace in London on ground that went on to become known as 'The Mall' and later Pall Mall – strange to think that a forerunner of croquet is responsible for the generic name of hideous 21st century shopping malls . . .

Another game with similarities to croquet was 'troco' or lawn billiards, which involved using a mallet to hit a wooden ball through an iron ring (as opposed to hoop) fixed to the ground. This was especially popular in Victorian times, which is when croquet first appeared on the social scene.

Modern croquet seems to have had two immediate forerunners, one being a mallet and ball game popular at spas in southern France. This was invented by a French doctor in 1832 as exercise for his patients and was indeed called 'croquet' – from the

French for 'crooked stick' apparently; the other possible root of the game is an Irish game called 'crookey', which was introduced to England in the 1850s.

Either way, croquet quickly became extremely popular, largely because it could be played equally well by both men and women, and eventually the Wimbledon All England Croquet Club (which went on to become the Wimbledon All England Tennis and Croquet Club – you may have heard of it . . .) was formed in 1868 as the headquarters of the sport in England. It was replaced as the organising body for the sport in 1898 by what is now the Croquet Association, after the new sport of tennis began to usurp croquet.

Up to then, mallet and ball games were played with crudely fashioned wooden balls with little standard measurement. Once the Victorians got their hands on the balls and codified the sport in 1867, however, this sorry state of affairs was soon set to rights. This is perhaps just as well since within 50 years of its introduction to England croquet had spread to all of Britain's colonies and elsewhere around the world, and was even an Olympic sport by 1900. The rules are not standardised globally, however. The Americans, for instance, have their own version, as do Japan and Egypt, but the variations are not enough that players of one game can't readily adapt to the other.

The first standardised croquet balls were made by the London firm of John Jacques & Co Ltd. Jacques continued to be a major supplier – and originator of the British rules – until their factory was destroyed by fire in 1997. Early balls were carved from a single block of Turkish boxwood with an oil paint surface, but Jacques replaced this in 1906 with their own coating known as 'Glisglos' and this remained pretty much the standard ball until 1945, when a new composite ball known as the 'Eclipse' was introduced. This had a cork (and later a solid plastic) core with a casing which was dipped in nitro-cellulose for additional protection against wear and tear, and it was milled in two directions to give the standard and rather attractive diamond patterned texture found on the surface of croquet balls. This reduces gradually to four small circles known as poles. There were around 50 cuts in each direction.

MODERN CROQUET BALLS

At the time of writing the following balls are approved by The Croquet Association:

Dawson 2000 International 1st Colours
Dawson 2000 International 2nd Colours
Sunshiny (CB16) 1st Colours
Sunshiny (CB16) 2nd Colours
Willhoite Xtreme 1st Colours

None of these are made in the UK, thus indicating that, as with so many other sports, England gave Croquet to the world, then the world showed us how it should be done.

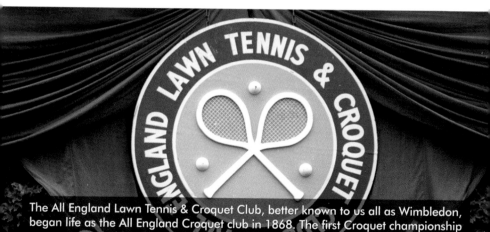

The All England Lawn Tennis & Croquet Club, better known to us all as Wimbledon, began life as the All England Croquet club in 1868. The first Croquet championship was held in 1870, seven years before Tennis came on the scene.

It became common practice for companies to engrave their mark on the poles. Jacques featured the company name, for instance, whilst South African manufacturer Barlow stamps a 'C' on one pole of their C ball and a 'G' on their GT model.

The Eclipse was an extremely popular ball, but had its faults – if crushed it could chip, crack or peel, and in hot, sunny climates black balls were even known to explode. Another British company, Ayres, produced a 'Championship' ball which was the worldwide favourite until they stopped production after WWII.

Large quantities of top quality UK-produced balls were exported after the war, allowing other British companies such as Slazenger and the British Composition Company into the market with composite balls, whilst later in the 20th century overseas manufacturers moved onto the scene.

Of these, Barlow of South Africa, Dawson of Australia, Sunshiny of Taiwan and Willhoit of the USA are now the biggest, with various production techniques. Dawson balls are made by the Australian Croquet Company and are manufactured from polyurethane in a two-piece mould, whilst Barlow use a solid nylon core and casing, and the width of the milling may vary from one manufacturer to another.

Whilst a croquet ball may appear as a rather heavy and unwieldy sphere in comparison to most other sports balls, it nevertheless has to pass some pretty rigorous tests to be accepted for serious competitions.

Roundness is vital, of course. Sunshiny or Willhoite are generally considered the 'roundest' balls (if they are not sufficiently round croquet balls can stick between the hoops). Other tests include weight (better balls will show a variation of no more than 5g in 454g) and bounce, measured on six points of the ball.

Milling is also a vital feature since it affects how well the ball adheres to the mallet when struck. If the ball is made from soft plastic the milling must be deeper, which means that the ball is lighter and won't bounce as well as with shallow milling, and it may also affect the consistency of shots. In this respect Dawson balls are well regarded.

FOOTBALL

ON THE BALL

"We wyll playe with a ball full of wynde."
Translation from 1519 Latin textbook written by William Horman,
headmaster at Eton and Winchester colleges.

"The foteball strengtheneth and brawneth the whole body."
Richard Mulcaster, from Positions Wherein Those Primitive
Circumstances Be Examined, Which Are Necessarie for the
Training up of Children *(1581)*

"Hacking is the true football."
F. W. Campbell, first FA treasurer, tells it like it is.

"We're at the cutting edge of science here because we
understand more about the aerodynamics of airplanes and
Formula One cars than we do of spheres."
David James of Sheffield Hallam University's Sports Engineering
Department on the development of the Adidas +Teamgeist ball
used in the 2006 World Cup.

CURVE BALLS

Roman writer Cicero describes the case of a man who was killed whilst having a shave when a ball was kicked into a barber's shop.

Some 80% of the world's footballs are made in Pakistan, and 60% of the entire world's production comes from one city, Sialkot.

The testing programme for the Adidas 2006 +Teamgeist ball included repeated kicking by a robotic leg to replicate the 2,000-plus kicks it would endure in a typical World Cup match.

VITAL STATISTICS
FIFA approved standards:
      Circumference: 68.5cm–69.5cm.
      Weight: 420-445 gms (dry).
      Pressure: 60-110 kPa.

Water Absorption: No more than 10% weight increase
Loss of Pressure: Max. 2%
The standard ball is known as a Size 5

THE FOOTBALL

England has long since claimed to be the home of football, but sports based around the concept of kicking a ball or other spherical object date back several thousand years and can be found all over the globe.

There are records from over 2,000 years ago during China's Han Dynasty of a game called **Tsu Chu** (tsu – 'kicking the ball with feet'; chu – 'a stuffed ball made of leather') in which a **zuqui** was used – a volleyball-sized sphere made from stitched leather panels and stuffed with animal fur. This was replaced by an air-filled ball during the period of the Tang Dynasty (618-906 AD).

The Japanese were also playing a version of 'keepie-uppy' called **Kemari** around 2,000 years ago, which involved lots of yelling and shouting since players had to cry "Ariyaa!" every time they touched the ball, which was eight inches in diameter and made from deerskin stuffed with sawdust. It's possible that the first international 'football' match was played in around 50 AD between a Japanese kemari team and a Chinese tsu chu team. The score is unrecorded.

In North America, Native Americans were recorded in the early 17th century as playing a violent and rather busy game of 500-a-side football called **Pasuckuakohowog**, which translates as 'they gather to play ball with the foot'. Further north the Inuit enjoyed nothing more than a game of football on ice (still common in the lower divisions of the Scottish League) called **Aqsaqtuk**. This featured a ball made from animal hide and whale bones stuffed with wood shaving, moss, hair and feathers and in one instance, the goals are said to have been ten miles apart, which puts a whole new slant on the term 'away goal'.

Meanwhile, in South America, the Mayans developed their own version of footie as much as 3,000 years ago using a solid rubber ball weighing up to 20 pounds and some 20 inches in diameter. This was a game which, to concur with former Liverpool manager Bill Shankly, was more important than life and death since the losers were often sacrificed to the Gods.

It's OK. Marc-Antione Fortuné of West Brom hasn't been sacrificed and had his head replaced by a ball. Honest.

The Aztecs later played a similar game called **Tlachtli**, which also used a rubber ball – their priests considered that the movement of the ball during the game symbolised their future. This game actually bore some resemblance to American Football in that players often wore knee pads and helmets (partly for protection from the heavy rubber ball). Mind you, should you be defeated, body armour would be of little use for, like the Mayans, the Aztec Gods liked the taste of losers.

In Australia the Aboriginal people of modern day Victoria had their own version of football called **Marn Grook**, which used a ball made from the skin of a possum and may have had an influence on the development of Aussie Rules football as drop kicks and leaping to catch the ball, both features of Aussie Rules, played a major part in the game.

In Europe the Middle Ages saw various games develop that were loosely related to football – in Italy there was **Calcio**, in France **Soule** or **Choule**, both using a stitched leather ball stuffed with leather and bran and deriving from a Roman game called **Harpastum**, which was not strictly football since it allowed the use of the hands.

Across the Channel, England had seen foot-related ball games develop from the 8th century onwards, but with precious few rules. Games were often played between neighbouring towns and villages and may have had up to a thousand players ranging across a 'pitch' that could include the competing towns and the intervening fields and countryside. In true English footballing tradition, such games were violent, with not only physical injuries being very common but also damage to property, fields, hedges and fences. The ball was a rough and ready affair, usually made of an inflated pig's bladder encased in leather.

Partly due to its violent nature, but more because it took peasants and the lower classes away from both work and military training, football was banned on several occasions in the Middle Ages in England, viz, Edward III's edict in 1363:

A shop in Ashbourne, Derbyshire is boarded up re
for Shrove Tuesday's match between the Up'ards
the Down'ards, who attempt to score, using a
specially painted ball filled with cork, in goals s
three miles apart on the banks of the River Henm

"… we ordain that you prohibit under penalty of imprisonment all and sundry from such stone, wood and iron throwing; handball, football, or hockey; coursing and cock-fighting, or other such idle games."

Such old-style games are still held throughout the UK and elsewhere on holidays and festivals. Amongst these are Christmas and Hogmanay games at Kirkwall in the Orkneys and Duns in Berwickshire and Shrove Tuesday matches at Alnwick, Ashbourne, Corfe Castle and Sedgefield.

But it took more than a royal decree to prevent 'idle games' from flourishing in England. By the early 19th century football was so well established that there were semi-official rules, which featured a pitch 80-100 yards long and a goal made of two sticks a yard apart. It became popular in public schools with some, such as Rugby and Marlborough, preferring a game in which the hands could be used, whilst others, notably Eton, Charterhouse, Harrow and Westminster, preferred a 'feet only' version.

By 1851 William Gilbert of Rugby was exhibiting balls made specifically for football and rugby at the Great Exhibition in London. The Football Association was set up to officially codify the rules of the game with the first 'Laws of Football' being published in December 1863. There was much discussion over Rule X: 'any player shall be at liberty to charge, hold, trip or hack [his opponents]', which unfortunately didn't make the cut.

The original laws made no provision for the shape, size and weight of the ball, however, and it was not until 1872 that the FA decided that the ball, 'must be spherical with a circumference of 27 to 28 ins', whilst the 'weight should be 13-15oz' (this was increased slightly in 1937 to 14-16oz) and the 'outer casing should be of leather or other approved materials'. These weights and dimensions stand to this day.

However, there has been plenty of innovation within these parameters in terms of ball design and construction. One of the biggest steps forward – more of a toe punt really – was the construction in 1855 by Charles Goodyear of the first football with a vulcanised rubber bladder. This allowed standard-sized rubber bladders to be used inside leather balls, which maintained the size and shape of the ball, unlike the pig's bladder which had generally been used prior to this. There's also evidence that regularly blowing up a pig's innards by a human rather than machine could be harmful to health.

When the English Football League was founded in 1888, mass production of footballs kicked off in the UK, with one of the first companies to set up being Mitre. The best early balls were made from rump leather, cheaper balls from shoulder leather, and the skill of the cutters and stitchers was a major factor in how well a ball performed.

The ball case would be stitched inside out and then reversed so the stitching was on the inside (imagine heading a ball with the stitching on the outside), then an uninflated bladder was inserted through the slit.

The bladder was then inflated through a long aperture which was inserted through the small slit in the case, and then laced tight. These balls would soak up moisture and gain weight considerably, and this, along with the lacing, could make heading the thing a very painful affair – head and neck injuries often resulted. On top of all this it was pretty common for the balls to deflate during the course of a game.

Balls varied in shape and size in different countries, and it wasn't until after the formation of FIFA in 1904 that football dimensions became standardised worldwide. Ball construction also improved over time – in the 1940s, for instance, a cloth carcass was added between the outer and the bladder which helped to maintain the shape of the ball as well as providing a certain amount of dampening and additional strength, all of which allowed for improved dribbling, shooting and heading.

After WWII there was a dip in the quality of footballs due to the use of inferior leathers, with many bursting during the course of a game, as happened in both the 1946 and 1947 FA Cup finals, but from the 1950s onwards technological improvements came thick and fast.

The standard colour of the ball up until the 50s had been brown, although white balls were used unofficially as early as 1892, with the leather being whitewashed rather than dyed. But from the 50s white balls became more common as they were easier to see under the new innovation of floodlights, and orange balls were also introduced for improved visibility in snowy conditions.

Boris Becker and Vitali Klitschko take on the youth of Berlin at street soccer during the 2006 World Cup.

Attempts were also made to prevent water absorption, with various synthetics being applied to the ball's outer casing to repel water, and a new valve was introduced which did away with the need to have a laced slit on the ball.

However, the most obvious post-war changes came in casing design. In the 1950s the Danish company Select developed the now traditional 32-panel ball, which maintained a more spherical shape than the 18-panel design. The two vied for supremacy through the 60s, but after television viewers complained of the difficulty of seeing the ball during the 1966 World Cup, FIFA commissioned Adidas to develop a viewer-friendly alternative.

So it was that the now familiar black and white football was introduced in the 1970 Mexico World Cup, with 12 black pentagons and 20 white hexagons making up the famous **Telstar** ball.

Adidas has provided the official balls for all subsequent World Cups and this has obviously had an impact on the lower echelons of the game. Here's how the company used the event to develop their footballs:

1978 Argentina
Introduced the *Tango* design, consisting of 20 'triads' which created an optical illusion of twelve identical circles.

1982 Spain
Tango Espana, featuring waterproof rubber sealed seams – unfortunately the rubber tended to rub off in play and the ball often had to be replaced during the game.

1986 Mexico
Tango Azteca, the first fully synthetic football, which proved extremely effective in preventing water absorption.

1994 USA
Questra, manufactured from five different synthetic materials with a flexible and more durable polyurethane outer case.

2002 South Korea/Japan
Fevernova, featuring a syntactic foam layer and a three-layer knitted chassis for a more precise and predictable flight path.

2006 Germany

+*Teamgeist*, a high-tech thermally-bonded ball made up of 14 panels (replica balls have the 14-panel pattern superimposed on a cheaper 28-panel ball).

Of course, other companies besides Adidas have helped develop the football – for instance Nike's *Total 90 Aerow* has a pattern of rings, which is supposed to help goalkeepers determine the ball's spin (doesn't that give them an unfair advantage over strikers?).

But no football has had the high tech input that went into the +*Teamgeist*. Apart from an R&D programme that involved being booted to death by a robotic leg and immersed incessantly in water, the construction was a million miles away from the old leather cannonballs of the early 20th century. It consisted of two layers, while new thermal bonding technology produced a seamless surface, which promised a 'rounder' ball, enabling a player's foot to produce the same impact wherever it was hit, leading to a more consistent response from the ball. The lack of seams also meant the +*Teamgeist* didn't absorb water during a match.

Despite all the millions of pounds spent on developing it, goalkeepers hated +*Teamgeist*. "It's goalkeeper unfriendly. Very unfriendly," moaned England keeper Paul Robinson – but strikers loved it, as was evident from the many spectacular shots that hit the back of the net during the 2006 tournament. They were all over the moon.

And at the end of the day, whether it's a waterlogged leather brick or a high tech waterproof sphere, hitting the back of the onion bag is what it's all about. As well as being a game of two halves . . .

A FAIR DEAL

Most football fans probably share the author's resigned sense of dismay at the ludicrous wages the effete prima donnas of the Premier League command, so it's good to know that the balls these fops regularly fall over to claim unwarranted penalties could – if the Premier League had any sense of morality or ethics – be purchased from Fair Trade dealers. But since these two attributes have long been redundant in top flight English football it's unlikely we'll see Premier League players dribbling with a Fair Trade football any time soon.

However the rest of us can and should buy Fair Trade balls since it's a well established fact that many major manufacturers of footballs pay sweatshop wages to women and children in countries such as Pakistan to make their balls.

A top-of-the-range Fair Trade football such as the *Pro Ice* can be purchased for just £35.80, for which you'll get an 18 strip panel ball with an outer skin made from 'top-of-the-range micro-fibre-PU and an inner construction of four-ply woven polyester lining and balanced latex bladder'. You quite literally can't say fairer than that.

You'll also be pleased to remember as you punt your ball around a muddy English field that it was stitched by 18-year-old Sameena Nyaz who works at the Talon football stitching centre in Chak Gillan near Sialkot, the world capital of football production. Talon were the first Fair Trade football suppliers and Fair Trade are the only buyers who pay enough for workers to provide their families with all the basic necessities.

Are you listening Adidas, Nike and co?

Life's a beach: 'exotic' actresses play beach football on behalf of Austria and Germany, 'wearing' their national colours.

A FEW (FOOT)BALLS UPS

A Brazilian referee left the match he'd been officiating on horseback and at a swift gallop after shooting dead a player who disputed a penalty decision.

In 1979 a Scottish Cup tie between Falkirk and Inverness Thistle was postponed 29 times because of bad weather.

The Isles of Scilly has only two football teams, the Gunners and the Wanderers. They play each other every week in the league, and also meet in cup-ties.

The Albanian national team left the UK in disgrace in 1990 after a stopover at Heathrow, where they went on a literal free-for-all in the airport's shops believing that 'duty free' meant 'help yourself'.

Pedro Gatica cycled from Argentina to Mexico for the 1986 World Cup, but couldn't afford to get in to the matches, so he set about haggling for a ticket. Whilst doing so his bike was stolen.

Danish referee Henning Erikstrup was about to blow full-time whilst officiating at the Norager versus Ebeltoft Danish league match when his dentures fell out. While he was searching for them Ebeltoft levelled the score to 4-4, but despite protests from Ebeltoft the referee disallowed the goal, popped his teeth back in and blew the final whistle.

Romanian midfielder Ion Radu was sold by Second Division Jiul Petrosani to Valcea in 1998 for 500kg of pork.

GOLF

ON THE BALL

"Golf is like chasing a quinine pill around a cow pasture."
Winston Churchill.

"I know I'm getting better at golf because I'm hitting fewer spectators."
Gerald Ford, former US President.

"The least thing upset him on the links. He missed short putts because of the uproar of butterflies in the adjoining meadows."
P.G. Wodehouse.

"One of the reasons Arnie [Arnold Palmer] is playing so well is that before each tee-shot his wife takes out his balls and kisses them."
A US TV commentator with perhaps the golfing gaffe of all time.

CURVE BALLS

Americans spend more than $600 million a year on golf balls.

The chances of making two holes-in-one in a single round of golf are around 67 million:1. In 1971 25-year-old pro John Hudson did just that at the 11th and 12th holes (195 yards and 311 yards respectively) in the Martini Tournament at Norwich.

Chances of making a single hole-in-one? Male pro or top amateur 3,708:1; female pro or top amateur 4,648:1; average golfer 42,952:1.

Rudyard Kipling painted his golf balls red so he could play in the snow.

Golf is the only sport ever played in space. In 1971 US astronaut Alan Shepherd took a 6-iron and a golf ball to the moon. His third shot (of three) is estimated to have travelled 1.4km thanks to the effects of zero gravity. The ball is still waiting to be found . . .

VITAL STATISTICS

Symmetrically spherical

Diameter: Min 1.680ins (42.67mm).

Weight: Max 1.620oz (45.93g).

Max velocity: 250 feet per sec.

THE GOLF BALL

The golf ball's history and its technological development is perhaps the best documented of all sports balls. The first golf balls, recorded as being used on the east coast of Scotland in 1550, were made from wood (as were the clubs). That said, although Scotland is generally acknowledged as the home of the sport, there are records of a similar game being played in China in the 11th century in the D ngxu n Records (and possibly as much as 3,000 years ago), whilst a game which involved hitting a leather ball with a stick into a target several hundred metres away was recorded in Holland in 1297.

But by the time the golf ball had become more sophisticated than a mere lump of wood there's no doubt that Scotland was the home of the game. Records show that the 'featherie' was introduced in 1618, this being a leather sphere packed, as the name suggests, with goose or chicken feathers. Skilled craftsmen in towns like golf-mad St. Andrews would stitch together a number of pieces of cow or horse hide, leaving a small opening into which was stuffed a 'top hat full' of boiled and softened feathers before the whole thing was stitched shut. Both feathers and leather were wet whilst this was done, and as they dried out the feathers expanded and the leather contracted to create a surprisingly hard ball that could be driven hundreds of yards by a skilled player.

The ball was also hammered into as round a shape as possible, coated with several layers of paint and punched with the ball maker's mark before being sold at a price which reflected the time and skill involved in the manufacture (and thus priced many people out of the game).

The featherie remained in use for well over 200 years, with the longest recorded drive being 361 yards by Monsieur Samuel Messieux in 1836 on St. Andrew's Old Course, although a typical drive was more in the region of 150-175 yards (compared to 180-250 yards with a modern ball).

In 1848 the 'guttie' was introduced by Rev. Dr. Robert Adams Paterson of St. Andrews. Made from gutta percha, a rubbery sap from the Malaysian sapodilla tree, the guttie was made by boiling the gutta percha until it became soft and could be handrolled on a 'smoothing board' into the correct size and shape. These balls were more resistant to water and cheaper to make than a featherie. They could be repaired by re-heating and re-shaping and thus, despite some opposition from traditionalists, gradually replaced the featherie as well as introducing more people to the sport. As with featheries, gutties were often stamped with the maker's mark, one of the most renowned being Allan Robertson, the first person to record a round of under 80 on the Old Course at St. Andrew's in 1859.

Interestingly, it was found that 'gutties' that were not smoothed after play travelled further and truer in flight, which led to the hammering of gutties with a sharp-edged hammer (famous exponents of this practice included Scottish club makers such as Gourlay and Auchterlonies). This was the forerunner of the dimpled ball – indeed by the 1880s balls were made in moulds that created patterns on the ball surface for this very reason. The best known and most popular of these was the 'bramble', so named because it looked similar to a bramble berry, with raised spherical bumps across the ball's surface, and this being the period of thrusting Victorian entrepreneurship it saw rubber companies such as Dunlop mass-producing golf balls which effectively saw the end of hand-crafted balls.

However, probably the biggest development in golf balls came in 1898 when the rubber core ball was invented by Cleveland, Ohio golfer Coburn Haskell, working in conjunction with the rubber company B.F. Goodrich. These balls were made from a solid rubber core wrapped in rubber thread and encased in a gutta percha outer, and looked pretty much like 'gutties' but gave the average golfer a good 20 yards extra length in driving from the tee. Shortly afterwards a thread winding machine was developed so that the balls could be mass produced, making them much more affordable, whilst in the early 1900s the gutta percha outer was replaced with a balata cover (balata is a similar material to gutta percha, derived from the South American bully tree).

Various outer patterns were also being developed to improve the flight of the ball, with dimples first being used in 1905 by William Taylor, and there was a wide variation in ball sizes and weights since there were no set standards at the time.

CUTE DIMPLES

Golf balls have dimples in order to allow the ball to travel further when struck. The dimples produce two layers of air around the ball, with the top layer travelling faster than the bottom layer, which creates turbulence. This in turn reduces the drag force of the air and allows the ball to travel further than a smooth ball.

The dimple size and number can be varied to affect the aerodynamics of a ball in flight. On average a British golf ball will have 330 dimples and an American ball, naturally enough, will have more at 336.

Patterns include multi-sized dimples on the same ball, dimples within dimples, and deep and shallow dimples. Maximum dimple coverage is desirable since it increases flight stability and gives golf ball engineers (yes, such people do exist) a greater ability to refine ball flight characteristics.

However the more dimples, the thinner the 'fret' area (the surface between dimples) and if this is too thin the frets may shear on impact with either the club or the ground and the ball will scuff.

Most golf balls on sale today have about 300–450 dimples, with a few balls having over 500 dimples. The record holder was a ball with 1,070 dimples.

All brands of balls have even-numbered dimples apart from the 'Srixon AD333' which has, as the name suggests, 333 dimples.

The handiwork of a golf ball engineer.

In 1906 B.F. Goodrich introduced the pneumatic ball, an interesting little number with a compressed air core which had the propensity to explode if it got too warm. Other companies innovated with materials such as cork, metal and mercury for the core, but the basic Haskell rubber core ball remained the ball of choice for most golfers right up to the 1970s, when Spalding introduced the two-piece Executive.

Interestingly, it wasn't until 1991 that standard dimensions for golf balls were agreed between the two main bodies in golf, the Royal and Ancient in Scotland and the United States Golf Association in the USA, which meant that for most of the 20th century golf was played with slightly different balls on either side of the Atlantic.

Sometimes a golf ball flies just that little bit too far. On this occasion it's Phil Mickelson who has got a tad over-zealous.

OFF THE TEE

Modern golf balls utilise all manner of space age materials such as silicone and rubber in their design, but essentially conform to one of the following types:

One Piece – a very basic, inexpensive ball used by beginners and on the driving range. Made from a solid piece of Surlyn with moulded dimples, it doesn't offer huge distance because of its low compression. (Surlyn is a tough thermoplastic sheet also commonly used in orthotics/prosthetics applications.)

Two Piece – a hard-wearing ball which has maximum distance and is thus the most popular choice for recreational golfers. Usually made with a solid, hard plastic core of high-energy acrylate or resin, which is covered by a tough Surlyn or speciality plastic. It has a firmer feel which gives a longer drive, but less control.

Three Piece – a solid rubber or liquid core covered by a layer of enhanced rubber, which in turn is covered by a durable outer such as Surlyn or balata. They offer more spin than a two-piece ball and are popular with better players.

Four Piece – these are the longest-hitting and softest-feeling balls, with a solid rubber core and two inner covers which transfer energy from the strike to the core to give the driver distance. The thin but durable urethane outer layer also offers mid-iron spin and provides a better feel on the green.

Which is all rather a long way from a lump of wood being tapped around wind-whipped Scottish links.

HANDBALL

ON THE BALL

"Muscle strength is a very important factor influencing throwing velocity."
One of the conclusions of a scientific paper on The Relationships between Throwing Velocity and Motor Ability Parameters of High-Performance Handball Players *by the Warsaw Institute of Sport.*
Tell us something we don't know, Einstein.

"It's a hybrid version of soccer, water polo and lacrosse."
US Handball team member Tom Fitzgerald.
We're not sure where the feet, swimming pool or sticks come in though.

"They play ball using the palm of their hand."
French author Rabelais (1494–1533) describing an early form of handball.

CURVE BALLS

There are at least a dozen versions of 'handball' played around the world.

Although a minority sport in the UK and USA, handball is the most popular ball game across Continental Europe after football.

Handball was introduced to the Olympics in 1936, for the Berlin Games – apparently at the request of one A. Hitler Esq.

VITAL STATISTICS
Diameter:
      Men and youths: 58-60cm.
      Adult women and males: 12-16 years 54-56cm.
      Male 8-12 years and female: 8-14 50-52cm.

Weight: Approx 16oz.

Pressure: 0.4–0.5 bars.

THE BALL

First things first – since there are at least a dozen different versions of 'handball' played around the world (see list below) what we're referring to here is Team Handball, as played in the Olympic Games, and especially popular in mainland Europe.

It's probably fair to say that handball's precursors are amongst the oldest in sport – hitting a sphere with the hands is as natural as kicking one, so it's highly likely that ancient civilisations would have batted a ball of some sort around as a form of recreation. Games such as **Urania** (stop sniggering) in ancient Greece and **Harpastum** in ancient Rome had aspects of handball about them (although the latter is also claimed by some to be an ancestor of football and/or rugby), whilst the medieval German game of **Fangsballspiel** apparently translates as 'catch ball game', so one assumes the hands must have been used.

Records also exist from medieval France of a handball-like game which involved batting the ball rather than throwing it (and is also regarded as a forerunner of tennis) whilst further afield similar games are known to have been played in ancient Egypt, among the Inuits of Greenland and in South America (there is no truth in the rumour that an Argentine version of the game is popular around Diego Maradona's home town).

It wasn't until the end of the 19th century that these basic handball games were organised and given rules, however, with three separate developments taking place at much the same time. In 1898 Holger Nielsen, a Danish Olympian and schoolmaster, drew up the rules for handball (or **håndbold** as it was known in Denmark) as an alternative to football (soccer) on the grounds that players using their hands had more control than they did with their feet and consequently fewer school windows would get broken. Apparently this was based on the rules of a local game called **raffball**, which translates to the delightful **snatchball**.

Another set of rules was published in Germany in 1917 – on the 27 October to be Teutonically precise – which were then updated in 1919 and used for the first international handball game between Germany and Austria in 1925. And yes Germany won.

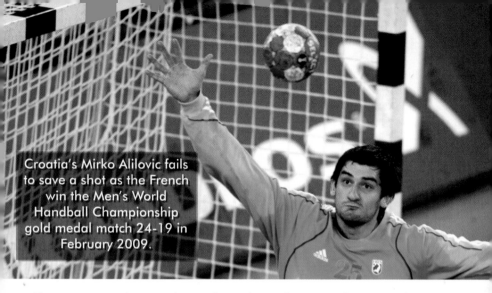

Croatia's Mirko Alilovic fails to save a shot as the French win the Men's World Handball Championship gold medal match 24-19 in February 2009.

The game proved extremely popular and growth was rapid. By 1928 the **International Amateur Handball Federation** was founded and by 1936 Handball had been introduced to the Olympics as an outdoor 11-a-side game, although it was dropped immediately only to be reintroduced in 1972 as an indoor 7-a-side game. The sport eventually moved primarily indoors (with a reduction in the size of the playing surface) to deal with the vagaries of the weather.

Remarkably little detail exists of the balls used in early handball, although early records of the game in Ireland indicate that the ball here was made of cloth wrapped in a leather case, but this was a version of the game more akin to American Handball (see P93).

The ball used in the early 20th century was essentially much like a soccer ball, although smaller, being made from leather panels stitched together with an inner bladder. This allowed the ball to be gripped and thrown.

A Yugoslav attacker makes an agile attempt on eventual silver medallists Norway's goal during the Seoul Olympics of 1988.

It was the Danish company **Select** who came up with a radical change in handball design in the 1950s – the 32-panel ball – which can still be seen today. This was also used for the company's footballs and resulted in the still familiar hexagonal panel pattern, which is able to maintain a more spherical shape than the previous 18-panel balls.

Select remain, along with **Adidas** and **Hummel**, one of the major handball manufacturers. Select's current range consists of synthetic and leather balls, with the manufacturing process described in loving detail on their website (**www.select-sport.com**). Interestingly the company claim that there is little difference in quality or playing characteristics between leather and synthetic balls. Their top quality synthetic balls, for instance, are used in the World Championships and Olympic Games, whilst their best leather balls are used in the world's top domestic handball league, Spain's Asobal League.

All Select's balls are hand stitched, with synthetic balls having a softer feel than leather balls and a better grip, so resin doesn't necessarily need to be applied to them. Their leather balls are made from finest top-grain croupon (butt) leather from the hide of young heifers, and resin must be used on them for grip – Select have a special and secret tanning process that allows the leather to absorb and hold the resin better.

Equally important is the bladder, made from latex, which the company claim is better than the other options of butyl or polyurethane as it retains better elasticity, bounce and shape. Apparently, they claim, a pumped up Select handball bladder will spring back to its original shape and size after being stood upon by a fully grown adult.

The softness of latex means the bladder better follows the curve of the inside of the ball, which in turn means there are no inner air pockets, allowing for better ball control and dribbling. Fascinating, and all very scientific.

OTHER TYPES OF HANDBALL

What I've described is Team Handball, but it's far from being the only form of 'handball', although it is the most popular. Other forms of the game from around the world include:

Gaelic Handball
in which players hit the ball against a wall with their hand instead of a racquet.

American Handball
similar to Gaelic handball, from which it originates.

Chinese Handball
a variant of American handball popular on the streets of New York in the 1960s and 70s.

Eton Fives
a hand ball game played in a few select English public schools.

Four Square
a game played on two or more squares and known as 'handball' in Australia.

New Zealand Handball
a tennis-style variation of four square.

Reverse Handball
popular in Australia, involving the use of external objects.

Keatsen
a Friesian version of handball played between two teams of three players.

ON THE BALL

"Field hockey is a crazy sport, anything can happen."
Barbara 'Barb' Marois, US Team member, makes a careful analysis of her chosen sport.

Seen on the net
'Top Ten Reasons to Date a Field Hockey Player'
from a female player calling herself 'Hockeygirlie'.

10) We work with balls really well
9) We can grip a stick
8) We do it for 70 minutes in 11 different positions
7) We like to be on top of our game
6) We enjoy getting hot and sweaty
5) We wear short skirts for easy play
4) We're used to getting our knees dirty
3) We always get called for third party
2) We know how to take it up the middle
1) We play until we score

So feminism is alive and well in the world of hockey . . .

CURVE BALLS

Early games of hockey at the world's first club, Blackheath in south east London, took place on a pitch at least 180 yards long, 60 to 70 yards wide and with a goal that was ten yards across.

The 'Indian Dribble' is not a problem encountered by masticating infants on the Indian subcontinent, but a revolutionary technique for using the stick perfected by Indian and Pakistani teams in the 1950s.

Hockey balls travel at such velocity when hit by a good player that goalkeepers are now required to wear almost as much padding as their counterparts in ice hockey, including chest protectors, upper body protection, a full mask and helmet and shin guards.

VITAL STATISTICS
Circumference : 224mm-235mm/8.81-9.25ins.

Weight: 156g-163g/5.5-5.75oz.

Material: Plastic.

THE HOCKEY BALL

Hockey is one of the many sports which claim to be the world's most popular team game after soccer, which makes it all the more remarkable that so little appears to be known by the game's authorities about the history of their ball; and at the time of writing one of the world's number one manufacturers of hockey balls didn't even have a website . . .

All the more of a shame since hockey has such a long history – or at least games which are clearly related to it do. Records of curved stick and ball games date back at least 4,000 years, with drawings from this period having been found in Egypt. There are also depictions of a hockey-like game from 2,500 years ago in Greece (where it was known as "Κερητίζειν" (pronounced 'kerytezin'). Ireland has enjoyed the closely-related sport of hurling (see p100) for at least 2,000 years, and a very similar game from Mongolia called 'Beikou' is at least 1,000 years old.

Hockey-style games were common throughout Europe in the Middle Ages, going under a variety of names – cambuca, clubbes, hurl-bat, shinnops, jowling, baddins, bandy ball and doddorts. Despite sounding like something out of a Harry Potter novel these were in fact medieval names for the game from various parts of England, whilst the actual word 'hockey' is probably of Irish origin, although it could also derive from the Anglo-Saxon 'hok' for hook, relating to the shape of the stick, or the French 'hocquet' for a shepherd's crook.

In typical medieval monarch style, 'cambuca' and 'bandy ball' were banned by both Edward III and Richard III in favour of archery practice, but the game prevailed until yet another gaggle of upper class Brits began to codify hockey in the late 19th century, before exporting it around the world like so many other modern team games.

By the time this came about, hockey in England was essentially a public school game which, rather amazingly, used a rubber cube rather than a ball. The heartland of early hockey was south east England, with the first club in the world being formed sometime between the late 1840s and 1861 in Blackheath. This may have been the handiwork of members of Blackheath Golf Club, which dates back to 1608 and in turn

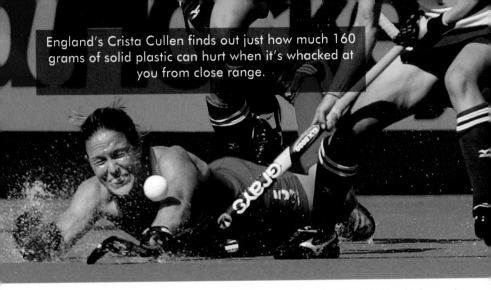

England's Crista Cullen finds out just how much 160 grams of solid plastic can hurt when it's whacked at you from close range.

claims to be the world's oldest golf club. They too played with a 'ball' which was in fact a cube of solid rubber, was designated 'not to exceed 7oz in weight' and which frequently had to be boiled to maintain its elasticity.

Later clubs included Teddington Cricket Club (despite the name the members played hockey as a winter training game), and it was here that in the first half of the 1870s someone came up with the rather spiffing idea of using a ball rather than a glorified Oxo cube to play. Not surprisingly the ball they went for was a leather cricket ball, which was painted white, but in all other respects was exactly the same object as they used in their summer game. Even today hockey balls have the same weight and dimensions as cricket balls.

Not all hockey clubs went along with the innovative idea of using a ball, however. When the Hockey Association was formed in 1886 by seven London clubs, Blackheath refused to join, stating that their version of the game was: 'so totally at variance with that adopted elsewhere.' Blackheath retained their rubber cube, along with other arcane additions to their own particular version of the game taken from rugby. These included scrimmaging, catching and marking.

Eventually Blackeath's idiosyncratic version was elbowed aside by what is essentially the modern game, although there have been countless rule changes since the International Rules Board, which later morphed into the International Hockey Federation, was founded in 1895. Hockey quickly spread worldwide, proving especially popular in British colonies, and indeed India and Pakistan were powerhouses of the game for many decades.

With the almost universal introduction of synthetic pitches for top level games in the 1980s came the only real change there has ever been in the hockey ball. Out went the old, seamed leather white cricket ball type ball and in came seamless, plastic balls. These were and are cheaper to produce, are more durable, have a more consistent behaviour on the playing field and are not affected by water – this is especially important since synthetic pitches are 'water-moderated'.

A modern hockey ball may be either hollow or have a core made from cork, rubber, injection-moulded polyurethane or, in the case of elite level balls made by a manufacturer such as Kookaburra, a quilted centre. The outer casing will be dimpled or plain plastic in various colours. Dimples were developed specifically for use on water-based astroturf pitches (although they're frequently used on any type of synthetic pitch) to help prevent the hydroplaning that can occur if a plain outer surface is used, as well as giving a more consistent ball speed.

A player from the late 1800s would have no doubt recognised the modern ball for what it is (unless they played for Blackheath), although the ball has a response that's light years away from that of the heavy old cricket balls of yesteryear.

HURLING

ON THE BALL

"The game was played on the white strand without shoes or stockings, and we went in up to our necks whenever the ball went into the sea. Throughout the Twelve Days of Christmas time there wasn't a man able to drive his cow to the hill for the stiffness of his back and his bones; a pair or so would have a bruised foot, and another would be limping on one leg for a month."

Author Tomás Ó Criomhthain describes a game of hurling on the remote Great Blasket Island off the coast of County Kerry in the first half of the 20th century.

"Pat Fox has it on his hurley and is motoring well now. But here comes Joe Rabbitte hot on his tail. I've seen it all now – a Rabbitte chasing a Fox around Croke Park!"

Radio Telifís Éireann commentator Mícheál Ó Muircheartaigh.

"1-5 to 0-8 . . . well from Lapland to the Antarctic, that's level scores in any man's language."

It's that man Ó Muircheartaigh again . . .

CURVE BALLS

An English hurling team, London Gaelic Athletic Association, won the 'All-Ireland' Senior Hurling Championships after beating Cork in the 1901 final. Irish revolutionary leader Michael Collins later played for the club, which still competes in the event.

After the introduction of new rules in 1999 referee Niall Barrett handed out 14 yellow cards and sent off 6 players in one Irish league game.

During the 1935 All-Ireland semi-final the ball ricocheted off a post and went into the stand. Embellished as it may be, the story is that the action on the field of play was so tempestuous that it was 22 minutes before any of the players noticed.

Irish hurling is not to be confused with Cornish hurling, also known as 'hurling the silver ball'. The Cornish version is a passing and possession game played with a small sterling silver ball (a sterling silver cover over a core of cork, leather or wood), but no sticks.

A good strike with a hurley can shift the ball at up to 150kmph (93mph).

VITAL STATISTICS

According to the Gaelic Athletics Association:

'The circumference of the hurling ball (sliotar) shall be between 23cm and 25cm. The ball weight shall be between 110 and 120g. The rib shall not exceed 2.4mm and shall not be less than 2.2mm.

The thickness of the leather cover shall not be less than 1.8mm. The leather cover shall conform with the designated Irish standard. The use of laminated splits, laminated corrected grain, or laminated full grain leathers shall be excluded.'

THE SLIOTAR

Whilst hurling has obvious links with hockey and other stick and ball games, it's Irish to its roots and one of the oldest stick and ball games on the planet, having been played on the Emerald Isle for over 2,000 years.

Hurling's closest links are to the similar ancient games of 'Bandy' in England and Wales, 'Cammag' on the Isle of Man and 'Shinty' in Scotland. It features in various well-known Irish folk tales, although the 'golden age' of hurling is generally regarded as being the 18th century, when Anglo-Irish gentry kept their own teams (somewhat like Russian oligarchs and Middle Eastern potentates in today's Premier League) which played regular games against each other.

Things went downhill somewhat after that, although the British obsession with codifying sports in Victorian times seems to have spread across the Irish Sea with the foundation of the Irish Hurling Union in 1879 and the Gaelic Athletic Association in 1884, which successfully set about getting the game back on its feet.

The world's fastest field team game (apparently) is now Ireland's second most popular sport after soccer and has been exported with limited success to Britain, North America, Australia and New Zealand.

The ball used in hurling is known as a 'sliotar', pronounced 'slitt-er', while the name 'hurling' comes from the stick, called a 'hurley' or 'hurl'. Hurling has never been a game for pansies, the more so in the past when the ball was sometimes made of hollow bronze, or a wooden core wrapped in leather. More humble matches may well have been played with a ball made of a bound mix of wood, rope and animal hair.

The sliotar eventually progressed to something a little less like a projectile and more like a sports ball, being made from a solid horse hair core with an outer surface made from two halves of leather stitched together. The seam of the stitching was and still is quite pronounced, which allows players to catch the ball more easily and also to run with it balanced on the hurley.

However, these early (pre-20th century) balls were still far removed from modern sliotars. They weighed more (the minimum prescribed weight at the time was seven ounces, which is around twice the weight of a modern ball) and tended to become even heavier when wet as the leather was not water resistant and the horse hair core soaked up moisture too – and remember this is Ireland which means they were wet most of the time. They also lost their shape, and being brown couldn't easily be seen in the quagmire that a hurling pitch becomes in the depths of winter.

Consequently, in the first half of the 20th century sliotars became more consistent in their manufacture for the benefit of both players and spectators. This was largely due to the work of hurling player and sliotar mender Johnny McAuliffe of County Limerick, who introduced a cork core with a better quality two-piece white tanned

Hurling: no game for pansies

pigskin outer. It was lighter (in keeping with current GAA specifications), maintained its weight and shape better due to improved water resistance and core, and had a far surer flight when struck. This all made the sliotar more visible to both players and spectators.

The compostion of a modern sliotar is now a cork core wrapped in a two-part leather cover, stitched together on the outside. There have been variations such as the introduction of a rubber-cored ball by sliotar manufacturer O'Neills a few years ago. However, this travelled faster and was a lot bouncier than cork-cored balls and was eventually abandoned as it gave players too many problems with control.

Despite improvements in manufacturing techniques and materials, controversy still rages over sliotars. They are renowned for varying in terms of shape, weight, water absorbency and the size of the stitching ridges, all of which can affect everything from a player's ability to strike the ball accurately to catching it. Since several balls may be used in any one game any differences are likely to be noticed markedly by the players.

As former Cork All Star goalkeeper Ger Cunningham has pointed out, "The variations were incredible . . . especially with the rims. The thickness of the rims would burn the hand off you if the ball was hit hard . . . other balls react differently to wet conditions, some lose their shape quickly. But most players will tell you it's the thick rims they object to most . . ."

Pat Daly of the Hurling Development Committee acknowledges, "This is not a science by any stretch of the imagination." But then maybe that's a good thing – if it was it would be called Formula 1 and how boring is that?

PÉTANQUE

ON THE BALL

"The game of boules is an attractive gymnastic exercise, an amusement of skill and spirit."
Aimé Coussin, Paris in a late 19th century document on the rules of the game in typical flowery French.

"Without doubt, this tournament will help to strengthen friendship and peace between people of the whole world."
Gassam Ezzedine, head of the local Pétanque Federation, expecting great things from the game at the start of the 2008 World Pétanque Championships in Dakar, Senegal.

"Things got out of hand and I found myself pinned to the wall with a sickle at my throat."
Patrice Joliveau, president of the Pouguès-les-Eaux team after a wee incident in a Pétanque game. 'Bouliganisme' strikes, as the Times *put it.*

CURVE BALLS

If you win a game 13-0 you are said to 'fanny' ('metre fanny' in French). From this for some reason has come the popular image in Provençe of a bare-arsed girl named Fanny whose bum losers must kiss. The lack of girls called Fanny willing to reveal their nether regions to rubbish petanque players has led to the tradition of having a substitute picture, carving or pottery image of a girl's bum at Pétanque courts for losers to plant a kiss upon.

The birthplace of Pétanque, La Ciotat, is also famed for the public screening of the world's first movie by the Lumière brothers in September 1895 at the world's first public cinema, L'Eden.

Boules features regularly in French art and culture. The artist Meissonnier painted images of the game, a match is described in Honoré de Balzac's *La Comédie Humain* and Marcel Pagnol features 'jeu de provençale', a forerunner of the game, in his memoirs. All of these are no doubt familiar to readers . . .

VITAL STATISTICS

Unusually and perhaps uniquely in ball sports, nothing about the boule is fixed. Its diameter is allowed to be varied so that it can be based on the size of the player's hand. The weight and 'hardness' (which depends on the material the boule is made of) can also vary and usually depends on the player's preference and playing style. 'Pointers' (players who throw the boule towards the jack) tend to choose heavier and harder boules, while 'shooters' (players who prefer to throw their boule at the opponent's boule to knock it out of play) tend to use lighter and softer boules.

Additionally, competition boules as used in Pétanque must meet the following specifications:

Be made of metal.

Bear engravings indicating the manufacturer's name and the weight of the boule.

Have a diameter between 70.5mm and 80mm.

Have a weight between 650g and 800g.

Not be filled with sand or lead, or be tampered with in any way. In addition, a boule may bear an engraving of the player's first name, initials or logo.

Leisure boules

As the name suggests these are not used for competition play and can be made of various materials, including metal, wood and plastic.

Competition jacks must meet the following specifications:

Be made of wood or synthetic material.

Carry the maker's mark and have secured confirmation by the F.I.P.J.P. (Fédération Internationale de Pétanque et Jeu Provençal) that they comply with the relevant specification.

Have a diameter of 25mm-35mm.

Additionally, painted jacks of any colour are allowed.

THE BOULE

First off you should perhaps know that 'boules' is the collective name for games played with metal balls, amongst which are Pétanque, the Italian game 'Bocce' and the Dutch game 'Klootschieten'. Since Pétanque is the best known and most popular of these, that's what we'll be looking at here, and when we refer to boule or boules we're referring to the metal balls used in the game.

The name Pétanque originates from the Provençal dialect phrase 'les peds tanco', meaning feet together, which describes the stance when throwing the boule at the jack, or cochonnet, a small wooden ball.

Pétanque has a relatively short history, its roots going back only as far as 1907 when it was apparently 'invented' by a M. Jules le Noir at La Ciotat on the coast of Provence in southern France. Earlier forms of the game had involved running before delivery of the ball, but apparently M. Lenoir suffered from rheumatism and was unable to do so – consequently he invented a variation of the game to take account of his affliction in which the delivery was made whilst standing still, and the pitch length was shortened by about 50 per cent.

On the other hand there's the story that it was invented by the brother of a bloke who had lost his legs in an accident and by having a stationary delivery and a shorter pitch, said brother was able to enjoy the game again . . .

Either way, versions of Pétanque have been around for thousands of years. There are records of the Romans adapting an earlier, sixth century Greek game which had involved throwing stone balls as far as possible by adding a target, and this was brought to Provence as their empire expanded. Wooden balls eventually took the place of stone balls as they were easier to manufacture.

A game similar to boules and known as 'globurum' was popular in the Middle Ages before being banned in the 14th century by French kings Charles IV and Charles V in much the same way as English kings of the same period banned bowls, football and pretty much every other form of fun the peasantry may have indulged in.

It doesn't get much more French than Cantona and Pétanque.

However, in the 17th century the ban was lifted and boules re-emerged to become one of the most popular games in France, particularly in the Provençe region where it was known as 'jeu provençal'.

Wooden boules were still used at this time, although these were often adapted by hammering iron nails with large round heads into the wood to add weight. Later, flathead nails of different colours and materials were used to create remarkably intricate and attractive designs and patterns. As Mike Pegg, President of the English Pétanque Association and the UK's only international umpire points out, "These boules were larger and heavier than modern boules – from 100 to 150mm in diameter and up to 1.5kg in weight. The makers became real artists, using nails of different metals (steel, brass and copper) to set out different designs such as symbols, numbers and letters, but also stars, flowers and hearts according to the wants of the players."

The game of jeu provençal was undoubtedly the forerunner of modern Pétanque, with the main difference between the two being that whereas in jeu provençal players run three steps before delivering the ball, in Pétanque they remain stationary. The dimensions and weight of the boules for both games are the same, however.

From its invention in 1907 it was only a matter of weeks before the first fully organised Pétanque tournament took place outside a café in La Ciotat, and the sport's popularity grew remarkably rapidly over the following decades until now Pétanque is by far the most popular form of boules worldwide.

Early games were played with wooden boules, but in 1923 Vincent Mille and Paul Courtieu came up with a set of boules made of cast bronze. This was followed five years later by the invention of steel boules by Jean Blanc, a blacksmith from the village of St. Bonnet le Château who devised a means of joining the two halves of a boule together. He sold these from the village ironmongers, and for about ten years steel boules competed with wooden boules for popularity, eventually taking over in the 1940s as the main type of boule in use. Today all boules are essentially hollow steel spheres and not surprisingly the majority of F.I.P.F.P approved boules manufacturers are based in France, although with the constant spread of the game's popularity, companies in Italy and Thailand have recently been given approval to manufacture competition boules.

One of the top manufacturers is the originator of steel boules, JB Boules in St. Bonnet le Château, who have now been making steel boules for over 80 years. Amongst their top end products is the 'JB 110 Soft Competition Boule' (£52 each), made from soft carbon chrome-plated steel with a 'velours titane' finish for better grip. Apparently it shouldn't be put away wet and requires regular cleaning and oiling to prevent oxidation.

And if money is no object a mere £135 will get you a 'JB Quatre X' with your name embossed onto the surface during manufacture (for an extra fiver). This semi-soft, stainless steel boule has been specially adapted, treated and tempered and has a brushed gold-coloured finish (although this eventually wears off during use). As the company's top-of-the-range boule it has 'advanced dynamic qualities, low bounce, straight trajectory and low levels of surface marking'. Top notch.

RUGBY

ON THE BALL

"It is a strange sight to see a thousand or fifteen hundred naked men to concur together in a cluster in following the [ball] as the same is hurled backward and forward . . ."
Historian George Owen (1552 -1613) describing 'cnapan', a Pembrokeshire forerunner of rugby.

"Rugby is a game for the mentally deficient. That is why it was invented by the British. Who else but an Englishman could invent an oval ball?"
Peter Cook.

"I couldn't very well hit him could I? I had the ball in my hands."
Tommy Bishop, former Great Britain rugby league captain when questioned about kicking a fellow player.

CURVE BALLS

Western Samoa's first international was against Fiji in 1924 – there was a tree in the middle of the pitch and the game kicked off at 7am so the Samoans could go to work afterwards.

Morley RUFC remains a bastion of unionism in the heartland of league as a result of the club's two representatives missing the 1895 meeting in Huddersfield which saw the split from union – they decided to stop off for 'a drink or two' en route to the meeting and consequently missed their train.

An Australian rugby player who complained of headaches and lethargy for some weeks after a game then suffered a head injury which required examination – upon which it was revealed he'd had another player's tooth embedded in his skull for over two months . . .

VITAL STATISTICS

As defined by the International Rugby Board a competition size 5 rugby union ball should have the following dimensions:

Shape: Oval, constructed of four panels.

Length in line: 280-300mm.

Circumference (end-end): 740-770mm.
Circumference (in width): 580-620mm.

Materials: Leather or suitable synthetic material. It may be treated for water resistance and to provide an easier grip.

Weight: 410-460g.

Pressure: 9.5-10lbs per square inch.

Rugby League balls are essentially the same, also known as size 5, but are slightly smaller and more pointed, with the following dimensions:

Length: 270mm.

Width: 600mm.

Weight 383-440g.

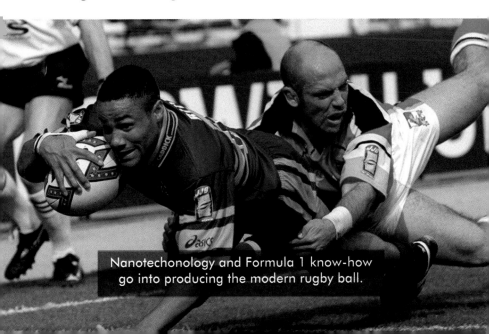

Nanotechonology and Formula 1 know-how go into producing the modern rugby ball.

THE RUGBY BALL

The 'invention' of rugby is famously credited to William Webb Ellis of Rugby School in Warwickshire, who in 1823 picked up the ball at a school football match and ran with it between the goals. Although a form of football in which handling was allowed had been played at the school since 1750, this was regarded as taking things a bit far and Webb Ellis was accused of cheating and consequently 'held in low regard' by many of his fellows; it was nevertheless possible for him to get away with it because the rules were regularly changing and there was no real 'tradition' in the sport of football/rugby.

Unfortunately, colourful as this story may be, in all probability it's a myth . . .

True or not, this wasn't by any means the first time a ball had been both carried and kicked in a game. The Roman game of 'harpastum' involved using both hands and feet, and closer to home games such as 'cnapan' in West Wales, 'campball' (ooo, get him...) in Eastern England, 'hurling to goales' in Cornwall and the Atherstone Ball Game, also in Warwickshire and still played today, all date from medieval times and had aspects about them which were similar to rugby, i.e. a rabble of individuals careening around after a ball in a loosely organised riot.

Webb Ellis' probably fictional move may have essentially been 'illegal', but by 1845 Rugby School had produced its first set of rules for the handling game. Prior to this, 300 or more players would take part in a 'match' – in effect the entire school – but as rugby spread to university and town clubs it was clear that more organisation was needed.

The first balls made specifically for the sport were constructed in 1832 by William Gilbert (1799-1877), shoemaker to Rugby School, who in 1842 moved to premises located next to the school.

Ironically, these days one of Gilbert's major competitors, Webb-Ellis, is based opposite Rugby School and also houses the small and rather homely Webb-Ellis Rugby Football Museum – if you're in the area it's well worth a visit. You may even catch ball maker John Batchelor in action producing hand-made leather balls. If you do, engage him in conversation to enjoy some splendid rugby tales.

There were no hard and fast regulations for rugby ball construction in the early days, and the reason behind the ball's 'prolate sphere' shape is that the pig's bladder from which they were made took on this shape when pressurised, although it has to be said that the shape does allow for far easier handling and passing than a true sphere would.

According to Mr E.F.T. Bennett, who played for Rugby School in the mid-1800s, 'The shape of our ball came from the bladder and was a perfect ball for long drop kicking or placing and for dribbling too . . .' It's difficult to imagine how dribbling with a roughly-shaped prolate sphere could ever be easy.

Early games used a bladder filled with paper or straw and no two balls were ever the shame shape, size or weight. Later developments saw balls being made from four pieces of cowhide stitched together and inflated by a pig's bladder on the inside. The bladder would still be green and smelly and was inflated by human lung power, through the stem of a clay pipe inserted into the bladder, which can't have been a nice job.

In 1870, Richard Lindop, a former pupil at Rugby School who also supplied his alma mater with balls, invented an inflatable rubber bladder which was both easier to blow up and helped prevent illnesses caused through inflating a 'raw' pig's bladder by lung power. His own wife had become ill as a result of blowing up her husband's balls . . . ahem. Around the same time an 'inflator' or pump was also developed, based on an enlarged ear syringe, which is the origin of the widely-used pump we know today, most commonly used for bicycle tyres and balls.

In 1871 James Gilbert exhibited the Rugby School Football at the Great Exhibition in London under 'Educational Appliances' and consequently exported 20 dozen balls to Australia. It was largely due to Gilbert's promotional work that the family business went on to export balls to the other colonies in the late 19th century, including New Zealand and South Africa, thus prompting the game to take off there.

In the same year the Rugby Football Union (RFU) was founded and in 1892 it introduced standard dimensions for the ball and made four panels the 'official' construction technique – prior to this six and eight panel balls had also been produced.

THE FIRST STANDARDISED RUGBY BALL

Dimensions:
- Length: 11 to 11¼ ins.
- Circumference (end to end): 30 to 31 ins.
- Circumference (in width): 25½ to 26 ins.
- Weight: 12 to 13oz.
- Hand-sewn with 8 or more stitches to the inch.

In 1893, the weight of the ball was increased from 13oz to 14½ oz.

Materials for the ball's outer covering varied, with Gilbert using both camel and pig skin as well as cowhide. The former two were found to be easier to work with, but were not popular with players since they became slippery when wet – which in the UK is obviously most of the time.

Meanwhile one of their employees, Henry Timms, who made some 50,000 balls between 1890 and 1935, introduced the technique of dry leather stitching. Prior to this balls had been made up 'wet' and had to be dried out before being despatched to market, but this new method meant balls could now be shipped to the ever-increasing domestic and overseas market immediately.

By this time rugby had split into two codes, union and league. This came about mainly as a result of the RFU enforcing amateurism on the game – fine for well-heeled former public schoolboys from the (predominantly) south of England, but a harsh imposition on the working class northern clubs whose players relied heavily on 'broken time payments' in order to take time off work to play the game.

Despite the fact that little love is lost between followers and exponents of the two codes, there is very little difference between the balls used by union and league. The latter balls are slightly smaller and have traditionally been six panels as this gives a more 'pointy' shape which is better for kicking, although today four panel balls are more common. To quote Tony Collins, professor of the social history of sport at Leeds Metropolitan University, "The only thing the two sports really have in common is the shape of the posts and the balls".

The need to have a ball that was easier to handle saw the dimensions of the union ball reduced by an inch and the weight raised by 1.45 oz in 1932, although different nations had their own design preferences. For example, the Kiwis and Aussies preferred more 'torpedo' shaped balls, while South Africans went for eight panels which offered better grip and the Home Nations stayed with four panels.

Gilbert remained the main brand for both union and league right up to the 1970s, with the Gilbert Match ball, made from cowhide, becoming the standard issue for union internationals in 1960. Indeed Gilbert remained with natural leather as other companies moved on to various synthetics and laminates that reduced water retention and, through use of round pimples for grip, allowed better handling, which may be one reason their popularity declined.

Companies such as Webb-Ellis (who supply the Heineken League and Welsh Rugby Union) and in rugby league Steeden, from Australia, are the other major players in the market today (Steeden so much so that the company name is often used generically in Australia for a rugby league ball). Gilbert also saw a revival such that by the 90s they were supplying the official World Cup ball (and still are) in the form of the Gilbert 'Xact'. This is a synthetic and laminate ball which uses a patented star-shaped grip pattern for better handling.

A modern rugby ball is a complex composite of modern materials technology. Gilbert's 'Synergie', for example, was developed through research with some of the world's top players along with computational fluid dynamics analysis (no, I don't know what it means either) and high speed video analysis. Even the valve is a technological masterpiece these days – no clay pipe stems and slimy pig's bladders here, thank you very much.

Webb-Ellis match balls combine nanotechnology and 3D modelling to determine the optimum shape and placement of the 'pimples' for minimum drag and maximum travel; they use an advanced rubber compound utilising Formula 1 tyre wet grip technology; and the bladder creates extra pressure at each end of the ball to give a better sweet spot and more accurate kicking over greater distances.

THE STEEDEN RUGBY LEAGUE BALL

A complex eleven-step process is involved in the creation of Australia's ball:

The outer is a special chemical composition made up of ingredients from several different countries which are mixed and then cured in a process that can take up to three weeks.

After curing, the material is then bonded with synthetic fibres to create the correct balance between tension and shape retention.

Next the grip is carefully thermo-moulded onto the material, then the ball is cut by both lasers and skilled artisans.

Each panel is then inspected under strict guidelines to meet weight, shape, printing and balance specifications; batches of panels are then sent for in-house testing of strength, abrasion and printing prior to stitching by specialists who may only work on one particular model.

The ball is then measured and inflated, and once again measured and tested for air leakage, before finally being cleaned in a chemically engineered wash, deflated and shrink-wrapped ready for market.

SHOT PUT

ON THE BALL

"Some kinda greenish powder came out of it."
World record holder Randy Barnes tells it like it is after his favourite shot splits open.

"Somewhere inside that flabby body was an athlete trying to get out."
Commentator Stuart Storey on Britain's favourite shot-putter, Geoff Capes.

CURVE BALLS

It's a shot 'put', not 'putt', although the term is derived from the phrase 'putting of the weight', which was a major feature of Highland Games competitions.

SHOT PUT WORLD RECORDS - observe carefully

MEN
Outdoor: Randy Barnes (USA) 23.12m/75ft 10¾ins, Westwood, California, 20 May 1990.

Indoor: Randy Barnes (USA) 22.66m/74ft 4¼ins, Los Angeles, 20 January 1989.

WOMEN
Outdoor: Natalya Lisovskaya (Russia) 22.63m/74ft 3ins, Moscow, 7 June 1987.

Indoor: Helena Fibingerova (Czech) 22.50m/73ft 9¾ins, Jablonec (Czech Republic), 19 February 1977.

If you did indeed 'observe carefully' you'll have noticed that these records have lasted some considerable time – in fact distances, especially for women, have decreased in recent years. You may also note that drug testing programmes have become more stringent in recent years . . .

VITAL STATISTICS

Track and Field
Men's shot – weight 16 pounds (approx 7.26kg); diameter 4.3-5.1ins (110-130mm).

Women's shot – weight 8.8 pounds (4kg); diameter 3.1-4.3ins (95–110mm).

Senior boys throw a shot weighing 12 pounds (5.44kg) whilst girls and 'midget boys' (yes, really) use a put of 8.8 pounds (4kg), the same as women.

THE SHOT

One could argue a shot is not a ball at all, but since it's both round and is used in sport (and fits the dictionary definition of a ball), it makes the cut as far as we're concerned. And what is in theory just a heavy spherical lump has more to it than you might think.

For a start the shot's origins don't, as one might expect, date back to the ancient Greek Olympics, but to the 19th century Scottish Highland Games. The events in the Greek Olympics were based around military and combat skills, particularly obvious examples being field events like the javelin and discus – the shot would have been precious little use on a battlefield even if you could throw it world record distances.

However, the shot has been used in the Highland Games since time immemorial when it was (and still is) a stone or metal sphere thrown from behind a line. Then, as now, it could vary in size and weight. Since the object to be hurled will often be nothing more sophisticated than a rounded stone or rock, this necessitates the allowance of some variation in both weight and size, unlike in track and field events. Weights, for example, vary from 16-26 pounds for men and 8-18 pounds for women.

The field event shot put could be said to be Scotland's gift to modern athletics as the event derives from the Highland Games' version of the sport, with the obvious addition of a regulation size and weight for the sphere. Indeed, the word 'put' derives from an old Scottish term for 'thrust' and refers to the throwing action of a shot putter. 'Putting the weight' mixes both Scottish and English terminology since a 'weight' is an old English measure equal to 16 pounds, the same weight as the men's shot put in modern track and field events.

There is another related event at the Highland Games, known as the Clach Cuid Fir (Manhood Stone), which involves lifting a huge stone of over 100 pounds in weight either to a certain height, or onto a wall. You can enjoy this endearing spectacle whilst digesting Christmas dinner leftovers on TV's annual World's Strongest Man event. (The stone put event in Gaelic, incidentally, is known as the Clach Neart, which translates as Stone of Strength).

The old (non-Olympic) event is a bit of a dog's dinner in terms of records, since very different weights were used. We won't bore you with all the technical details other than to point out that some events included putting 16 or 22 pound shots, whilst others featured 16, 20 and 25 pound stones (and for a time in the late 70s the record for the 25 pound stone, held by Brian Oldfield of the USA and standing at 46ft 5ins, was greater than that for the 20 pound stone). And just to make things a little more complicated the bloody Aussies use a 26 pound shot in their sun-baked Highland Games.

In modern track and field events the shot is possibly the simplest of all sports 'balls', being made from solid cast iron or brass, whilst those for indoor meets are a little more technical, consisting of a plastic shell filled with fine lead shot. It was one of these that world record holder Randy Barnes somehow managed to break (see opening quote). Quite what the 'greenish powder' that came out of it was, nobody seems to know – probably some form of degraded lead shot.

But if the event itself is simplicity personified, the techniques involved in putting the shot are not as simple as they seem. This is not merely a display of brute strength – and there are rules to be remembered too. For a start, an athlete must enter and leave the seven-foot diameter throwing circle from its rear half otherwise a foul throw will be called. They must then put the shot from the shoulder, ensuring it isn't brought behind the shoulder and it must be 'pushed' into the air rather than thrown, with the arm thrust outwards and the thumb pointing down; it must land within an angle of approximately 30 degrees; and if they step outside the circle at any point they are disqualified.

Techniques involve one of three styles – the glide, the spin and the cartwheel (yes, literally). The glide originated in the USA in 1951, when Parry O'Brien developed a technique that involves facing backwards in the circle then thrusting off from one leg to turn 180 degrees in a gliding motion before launching the put. Ideally it will land with a satisfying thud and the dislodging of turf and grass several metres distant.

In the spin, which was developed by Brian Oldfield in the 70s, the thrower also faces to the rear of the circle, but spins around on the ball of one foot before placing the opposite foot into the centre of the circle, spinning on this again then placing the first foot towards the front of the circle whilst facing forwards to launch the put – assuming he or she isn't completely dizzy by this point.

As for the cartwheel, incredibly throwers can develop enough momentum by holding the put under the chin, performing a cartwheel and launching it into the stratosphere.

Professional male shot putters tend to favour the spin, with the glide being more popular at amateur level and amongst women, although the cartwheel has also gained favour in women's shot putting in recent years, particularly among more athletic, lithe types. Perhaps the traditional image of a steroid-fuelled 'female' Olympic champion may become a thing of the past.

Oh, and just in case we hadn't made it clear, the winner is the one who puts the shot the furthest. Told you it was simple really.

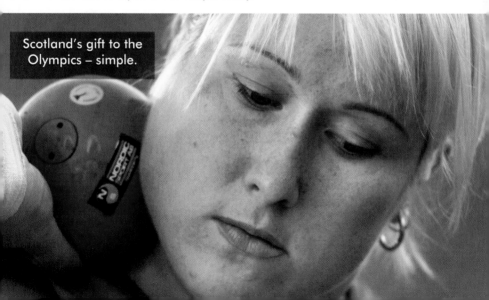

Scotland's gift to the Olympics – simple.

SNOWBALLING

ON THE BALL

So, you thought snowballs were randomly created and equally randomly-shaped lumps of snow you hurled at friends (and enemies) every winter as a child . . .

Think again. An 'official' snowball as used in the annual Showa-Shinzan World Snowball Championships in Hokkaido, Japan is between 2.56ins and 2.76ins in diameter, is produced in batches of 90 by a special machine, and is then used by one of 192 teams competing for the coveted world title (out of 2,000 vying for a place in the finals).

There's an 'official' pitch too, the same width as a tennis court, but twice as long, on which are placed four three-foot high walls behind which seven-man (or woman) teams can throw and shelter during the three-minute sets.

The aim of the game is not to get hit – if you are you're out. A team must win two sets to advance to the next round, and does so by having the most players left at the end of a set, or by snatching the opponents flag, located a precise 33-feet from either end of the pitch.

It should be emphasised that this is not child's play – top teams are sponsored by the likes of Sapporo Beer and will practise throughout the summer using imitation polyethylene 'snowballs'.

CURVE BALLS

As well as the Japanese, the students at Michigan Technological University in the USA seem to have a thing for snowballs – they rolled the world's largest snowball on 10 February 2006, a monster of 21 feet 3 inches in circumference, and on the same day 3,749 people got together for the world's biggest ever snowball fight on the university campus.

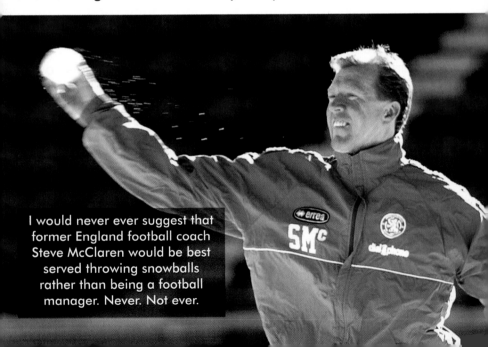

I would never ever suggest that former England football coach Steve McClaren would be best served throwing snowballs rather than being a football manager. Never. Not ever.

SOFTBALL

ON THE BALL

"When we played softball, I'd steal second base, feel guilty and go back."
Woody Allen

"If the Iraqi regime is able to produce, buy or steal an amount of highly enriched uranium a little larger than a single softball, it could have a nuclear weapon in less than a year."
George W. Bush – at least he knows how big a softball is.

"If history repeats itself, I should think we can expect the same thing again."
TV commentator during the Beijing Olympics softball competition.

CURVE BALLS

In October 2008 softball players in Kissimmee, Florida, had to rescue the pilot of a small plane who crashed after clipping their goalpost on take off.

Despite the use of underarm pitching, whirling-armed softball pitchers may reach speeds of over 70mph – indeed at the 1996 Summer Olympics one pitch was measured at 73.3mph (118 kph).

In New Orleans, a version of the game using a sixteen-inch ball called 'Cabbage Ball' is popular in schools.

Pitching at the Iranian Women's Softball Championships

VITAL STATISTICS

Circumference:
    Fast pitch: 12ins, +/- 0.125ins (30.5cm, +/- 0.3cm).
    Slow pitch: 11ins, +/- 0.125ins (29.7cm, +/-0.3cm).

Weight:
    Fast pitch: 6.25oz–7oz (178g–198.4g).
    Slow pitch: 5.875oz–6.125oz (166.5g–173.6g).

Balls may have a raised or non-raised seam.

The official colour in recent years for most standards of play is yellow, although traditional white balls are also allowed especially in the slow pitch game.

THE SOFTBALL

Softball should have a fairly straightforward history since it's a relatively new game with a well-recorded past. But history – even that of balls – is rarely straightforward.

Here's one version:

Thanksgiving Day 1887, Chicago, and alumni of Yale and Harvard Universities are gathered at the Farragut Boat Club for the results of the annual football game between their respective alma maters. When the scores are announced one of the Yale chaps chucks a boxing glove at a Harvard supporter in an early version of football hooliganism. The fellow who the glove was aimed it, using the kind of quick thinking and resourcefulness one might expect of a Harvard man, grabs a broom handle and hits the glove back. A second fellow by the name of George Hancock then ties another boxing glove to said stick thus creating a 'proper' bat and the first game of 'softball' takes place.

Within a week Hancock had developed a proper bat and ball and the Farragut Club came up with rules for the game, first published in 1889. It was initially known as 'indoor baseball', although within a year of being invented it was also played outside. This new game went on to spread rapidly – the same year as its invention a club was established abroad (fair enough it was only in Toronto, but it's still 'abroad'…).

Here's another version:

A few years after the high jinks in Chicago, firemen in Minneapolis were playing a similar game which went by the macho name of 'kittenball' after the team that invented it (the 'Kittens' not the 'Kittenballs'). This game was invented by one Lewis Rober, Sr. as an outdoor exercise for the fire crews and differed from the Chicago game in that the ball used was 12 inches in diameter rather than Chicago's 16-inch version, whilst also having a different-sized diamond. In a neat compromise, softball's regulation eventually utilised the Minneapolis ball and the Chicago diamond.

And here's a third version:

In 1916 some employees of the Atchison, Topeka and Santa Fe Railway in Kansas started to play a version of 'indoor baseball' in the limited space outside their employer's premises in Topeka. They used the same sized pitch as the indoor game, but a smaller ball of only 5.5 to 6 inches in diameter, which was so soft it was regularly smashed to pieces by the bat.

So a tougher ball was constructed – this involved rebuilding the core (records don't say with what materials), repacking the outer with hair and suchlike and sewing a tougher leather cover around it.

The problems with the balls falling apart continued as the game became increasingly popular, so much so that sporting goods manufacturers Spalding were asked for help. They produced a number of prototype models from which was chosen a ball that was smaller than an 'indoor' baseball but bigger than a regular baseball, and made from an elkhide cover with raised seams which had the purpose of protecting the stitching from being worn away by the bat and the playing surface. It was still soft enough that it could be fielded without the use of gloves, though.

These balls were sold by Spalding under the name 'playground' balls, just one of several early names for softball – others included the aforementioned indoor baseball and kittenball along with diamond ball, mush ball, cabbage ball and pumpkin ball, the latter three presumably related to the size, shape and feel of the sphere in question. With monikers like these it's perhaps just as well that Walter Hakanson of the YMCA eventually came up with the official name 'softball' at a 1926 meeting of the US National Recreation Congress.

By 1934 the name was standardised throughout the USA, as were the rules, and, whilst the USA remains the number one player of softball, it has been successfully taken up around the world, especially in Canada and Australia.

There are now well over 100 countries affiliated with the International Softball Federation, with an estimated 40 million softball participants worldwide, although, after being adopted in 1996, the game will not feature in the London 2012 Olympics.

Since the game became 'officially' recognised in the 1930s, the ball has changed relatively little. Up to 2002 it was usually made up of two pieces of white leather or synthetic material roughly the shape of a figure of eight and sewn together with red thread, whilst the core may be made of long fiber kapok, or a mixture of cork and rubber (these latter two particularly in the case of older balls) or a polyurethane mixture or other approved material. In 2002 traditional white leather was replaced by high visibility yellow casings.

It's nice to know that not everything in sport becomes standardised, however. In Chicago, where softball was invented, it's still common to play the game with an 'old fashioned' 16-inch ball which is softer than the standard 12-inch ball and consequently is sometimes called a 'mush ball', as in the old days. This size of ball is also used for wheelchair softball, and because it is softer fielders don't have to wear gloves when playing with it.

Major manufacturers of softballs today include Spalding (under the name Dudley), Wilson (under the name DeMarini, who manufacture slow pitch balls only) and Rawlings.

Just one thing, though – they're not really soft. But then you couldn't really call the game 'hardball' could you?

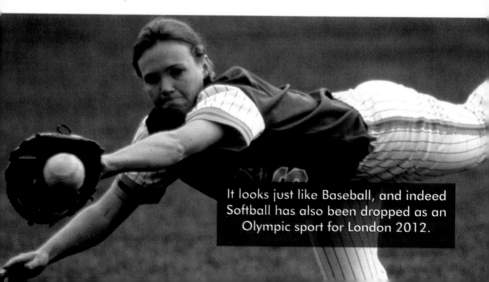

It looks just like Baseball, and indeed Softball has also been dropped as an Olympic sport for London 2012.

ON THE BALL

"Squash – that's not exercise, it's flagellation."
Noël Coward.

"Squash is boxing with racquets."
Six times British champion Jonah Barrington.

"I find that squash is less frustrating than golf, less fickle than tennis . . . easier than badminton, cheaper than polo . . . better exercise than bowls, quicker than cricket, less boring than jogging, drier than swimming, safer than hang gliding."
And more likely to get you a smack in the eye than any of them...
John Hopkins in Squash: A Joyful Game, *1980.*

CURVE BALLS

In the 2004 Canary Wharf Squash Classic, John White was recorded as having hit the ball at over 270 kmph (170 mph).

The spectacularly un-pc folks at Gradidge produced a ball in the 1920s called 'the nigger' – which besides being the obvious colour could also be purchased in red or white. Gradidge no longer exists as a company . . .

Squash is one of the best cardiovascular workouts you can get – in a one hour game a decent player may burn between 700 and 1,000 calories; it's also well-known for causing heart attacks amongst fat businessmen attempting to relive their youth.

Hole in one – the Avon India Rubber Company produced a squash ball in the 1920s which had a hole in it and was known as the 'Bath Club Holer'.

VITAL STATISTICS

Diameter: 40.0mm, +/- 0.5mm.

Weight: 24.0g, +/- 1.0g.

Stiffness: @ 23°C; 3.2N/mm, +/- 0.4N/mm.

Seam Strength: 6.0N/mm minimum.

Rebound Resilience – from 254cm @ 23°C; 12% minimum; @ 45°C, 26%-33%.

Colour of ball	Speed	Bounce
Double Yellow Dot	Extra Super Slow	Very low
Yellow Dot	Super Slow	Low
Green or White Dot	Slow	Average
Red Dot	Medium	High
Blue Dot	Fast	Very high

There is also an orange dot 'high altitude' ball.

THE SQUASH BALL

Yet again England provides the roots of another of the world's favourite sports. In this case we're in early 19th century Harrow School as the toffs come up with another way of having fun with their balls.

The sons of the privileged both here and at other public schools enjoyed racquets and fives, two sports which involved using a racquet to whack a small hollow rubber ball against the sides of a four walled-court, and noticed that when the ball was punctured it allowed them to play a wider variety of shots.

Playing with a 'squashed' ball took off and a new game was born. It soon became popular in other public schools and universities such as Oxford and Cambridge, to which public schoolboys progress as a matter of course, and by 1908 a committee had been set up to organise the sport.

Up until the 1920s there was wide variation in the size, weight and composition of squash balls. They were universally made from rubber, but, for example, the Avon India Rubber Company produced balls varying from 3.65 to 4.3cm in diameter with finishes which could be matt or varnished. The choice of ball for competitions depended on the size of the court until this was standardised, after which balls were also standardised.

From this point on, the ball became an integral part of the game, perhaps more than in any sport other than golf. A brief look at the online magazine *Squash Player* (www.squashplayer.co.uk) and their focus on their balls reveals this. Indeed, compare this with a sport such as handball where the regulatory authorities cheerfully admit to knowing nothing about the development of their balls . . .

But back to the 1920s, when the RAC were called out to be of assistance to the sport of squash – kind of. It was a member of the Royal Automobile Club in London, Col. R.E. Crompton who influenced what was then the Tennis and Racquets Association's Squash Rackets Representative Committee to adopt his club's standard ball for amateur championships after he spent time weighing, measuring and comparing the bounce of various different squash balls. One might say there was a vested interest on Col. Crompton's part, but then one would be a cad since he was clearly an officer and a gentleman.

Details on the ball, which was produced by the Silvertown Company and known as the 'Wisden Royal' (don't all these names just reek of Empire, Queen and country?) were lost in a fire at the factory in the Second World War, but it was given a run for its money by two additional balls, both produced by the India Rubber and Gutta Percha Company, which were 3 per cent and 5 per cent slower respectively ('slowness' of the balls is a fundamental aspect of squash which we'll come on to in a moment).

By 1926 the Tennis and Racquets Association had licensed further ball tests and laid down exact specifications for two squash balls to be used for competition play, marked 'T and RA – Standard' in red lettering and produced by Gradidge and Silvertown. The Squash Racquets Association replaced the T and RA in 1928 and used the Silvertown ball exclusively for championship games, whilst the Women's Squash Racquets Association, formed in 1934, chose the Gradidge ball.

The Second World War saw the end of Silvertown as a major player on the squash scene (indeed, it was difficult even to get new squash balls due to the scarcity of rubber and the fact that the major ball producers' factories were bombed), and after the war Dunlop became the major manufacturer, followed by Slazenger in the 1960s, who produced the first synthetic ball. This was made from butyl, a synthetic rubber which has the advantage that its performance is affected less by the temperature of the court, although it was not as resilient as rubber and balls would frequently split during a game.

Perhaps the most significant development for most players, however, was the introduction by Dunlop in the early 1970s of the coloured dot on balls to mark their speed, which made it far easier to choose a ball suitable for one's skill level. Dunlop still has the number one market presence in squash balls worldwide, and almost half of the world's top 50 players use the company's balls.

THE SCIENCE OF SQUASH

The manufacturing process of what at first appears to be one of the simplest of all sports balls is remarkably complex, as is the science behind it.

Dunlop squash balls are made from Malaysian rubber mixed with up to 15 different ingredients to produce the correct consistency for the particular speed of ball being made. Basically they consist of two halves of rubber compound glued together to form a hollow sphere then buffed to a matt finish.

The balls undergo a rigorous testing process to ensure they meet the permitted diameter, weight, stiffness, seam strength and rebound resilience required by World Squash Federation rules. This includes being compressed between two metal plates and pulled apart until the seam breaks.

The bounciness of a squash ball depends on the resilience of the rubber from which it's made, which is affected by all manner of things, not least of which is the fact that as the ball is whacked against the court walls the air inside it becomes pressurised which leads to the rubber becoming more resilient and the ball bouncing more.

In play the ball will heat up to around 45°C, when 'equilibrium' is reached and it plays at its best. This will depend to an extent on the temperature in the court and the skill of the players, hence the need for 'faster' balls (i.e. balls with less resilience) for less demanding players, indicated by the different coloured dots on the balls.

TABLE TENNIS

ON THE BALL

"Tennis is basically just ping-pong and the players are standing on the table."
Comedian Jerry Seinfeld.

"If you can't take a punch you should play table tennis."
Pierre Berbizier, French rugby union international player and coach.

"Ping pong is coming home."
Mayor of London Boris Johnson at the handover ceremony at the Beijing Olympics.

CURVE BALLS

Table tennis was the inspiration for the first commercially successful video game in the 1970s, Atari's 'Pong'.

Two players at the 1936 world championships in Prague took more than two hours to contest a single point.

Ping pong has also gone by other equally ridiculous names in the past including: Whiff Waff, Pom Pom, Netto, and Tennis de Salon.

The fastest recorded smash was a 112.5kmph howitzer by New Zealander Lark Brandt.

In 1988 table tennis became an Olympic sport, and it may well currently be the second most played sport in the world (be warned, you will read that claim elsewhere in this book . . .).

VITAL STATISTICS

Diameter: 38mm, 40mm, 44mm and 54mm are acceptable, although 40mm is the most commonly used and is the standard size for competitions.

Weight: 2.7g.

Colours: The choice of colour is made according to the table colour and its surroundings. For example, a white ball is easier to see on a green or blue table than it is on a grey table.

Stars: Stars printed on the ball indicate the quality, three being the highest.

Balls should bounce 23cm when dropped from a height of 30cm thereby having a coefficient of restitution of 0.88. Which, since you ask, is represented by:

$$C_R = \frac{V2_f - V1_f}{V1 - V2}$$

So there...

THE TABLE TENNIS BALL

The first table tennis 'balls' were made from the top of a champagne cork or a rolled up ball of string and were a feature of after dinner parlour games enjoyed by idle English toffs in the 1880s. A line of books across a dining table made up the 'net' and a cigar box lid or book would make the racquet to imitate 'regular' tennis.

At the same time game manufacturers were attempting to cash in on the increasing popularity of lawn tennis by manufacturing indoor games that mimicked the sport, with an 1890 set of parlour table games by David Foster in England featuring a 30mm cloth covered rubber ball and strung rackets.

The first actual use of the name 'Table Tennis' was on a board and dice game made in 1887 by J.H. Singer of New York which involved adapted rules of lawn tennis, whilst in 1898 London manufacturer John Jaques & Son Ltd. came out with 'Gossima' which used racquets, a 50mm web-wrapped cork ball and a 30cm high net.

Jaques re-introduced 'Gossima' in 1900, but under the new title, 'Gossima or Ping-Pong', the latter name being derived from the sound the ball made on the racquets which came with the game (if you ever see – and hear – one of these ancient sets in use you'll understand why, since the sound of a ball in play in a modern table tennis game sounds nothing like either 'ping' or 'pong'). That said, 'ping pong' had been in use along with various other nicknames for the game for some years prior to this. Eventually Hamleys of London trademarked the 'ping-pong' name and sold it to Parker Brothers in the USA.

Up to now all these games suffered from the fact that the balls were not very good – rubber balls bounced too much, cork balls not enough. However, this was the Victorian era and these were not people to be put off by a mere trifle such as the coefficient of restitution. In 1870 celluloid was registered as the first ever thermoplastic compound, and although it suffers from being highly flammable and also decomposes easily, when two hemispherical cavities of celluloid are joined together to create a sphere you get – hey presto! – the perfect table tennis ball (indeed, this is the most common use for celluloid).

This fact was discovered by English table tennis enthusiast James Gibb on a trip to the States in 1901, who saw such balls and introduced them to the game; in the same year E.C. Goode invented what we would now recognise as a table tennis bat with a sheet of pimpled rubber glued to a wooden blade.

Table tennis took off remarkably quickly, with the first (unofficial) world championships being held in 1902; the first national association being formed in 1921 in England (of course) as the Table Tennis Association, which was followed by the International Table Tennis Association in 1926; and the first official world championships in London in 1927.

Unlike so many other sports, relatively few technical changes have taken place in the table tennis ball – it still remains a hollow celluloid gas-filled sphere with a matt finish (usually white or orange), which is easily deformed but can be produced cheaply enough that this isn't a major problem.

Size-wise, 38mm balls were used in competition until 2000, when 40mm balls were introduced to make them easier for spectators to see, particularly on TV, since the greater diameter slows the balls down (the average competent player takes around 0.25 seconds to react to a shot, whilst experts will do so in 0.18 seconds or even less).

Ping pong ball grading varies from zero to three stars. A no-star ball is used for training or by novices, although one and two star balls are not considered good enough to use in competition and are rarely seen in use. For competitions a three or three star premium ball would be used for their consistent roundness, balance and bounce.

Arguably, no other sport places such a premium on the ability to spin a ball as does table tennis, but this is largely down to the composition of the rubber covering of the rackets rather than the ball. That said the small size and low density of a ping pong ball results in a bigger 'Magnus effect' than that of other sports balls – this is the name given to the physical phenomenon whereby a spinning object creates a whirlpool of rotating air or liquid about itself which helps to produce the various types of spin which are integral to the game.

The speed of modern table tennis doesn't appeal to everyone though, and some enthusiasts are looking to reintroduce the 'hardbat' game that existed before sponge rubber/reversed sponge rubber bat covers were introduced in the 1950s. The short-dimpled rubber of these bats decreases the Magnus effect of spin as well as the speed of the ball, resulting in more of a focus on the strategic side of the game as opposed to raw speed, reaction and strength.

Modern bats on the other hand have a combination of a thin layer of rubber with inward or outward pointing pimples on top of a sponge rubber layer, all laid atop a plywood/carbon/synthetic 'core' which combine to maximise the amount of spin and speed a player can produce, whilst the composition of the 'blade' itself affects the stiffness and the size of the sweet spot.

Another variation of the game which has resulted in slowing things down is 'large ball' table tennis using a 44mm diameter ball.

Whatever ball or bat you use, however, table tennis can be a remarkably good workout for a game that in essence involves standing on either side of a table tapping a ball across a tiny net.

Matthew Syed in his previous life as British Table Tennis Champion, before he became a *Times* columnist.

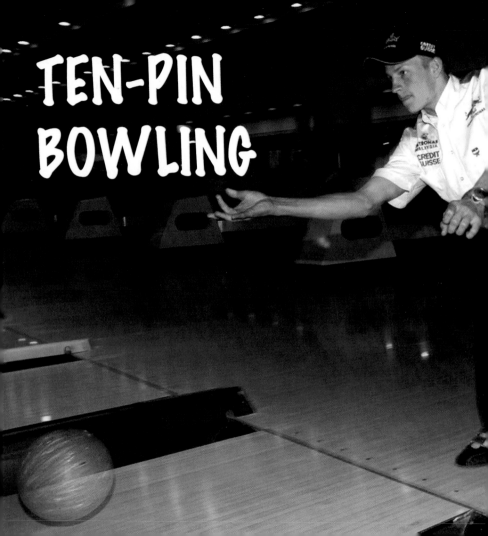

TEN-PIN BOWLING

ON THE BALL

"I haven't had sex in eight months. To be honest I prefer to go bowling."
Rapper Lil' Kim (who appears to have a couple of bowling balls attached to her chest) enjoying the rock and roll lifestyle to the max.

"The sport has become so sophisticated that knowledge of engineering and physics is likely to prove more helpful in throwing strikes than doing curls with a dumbbell."
John G. Falcioni in Popular Mechanics *magazine.*

"Are you embarrassed to be here?"
"On gay bowling night? Of course I'm embarrassed. But it's not the gay part that's embarrassing. It's the bowling."
Jen and Jack in TV show Dawson's Creek.

Maude Lebowski: "What do you do for recreation?"
The Dude: "Oh, the usual. I bowl. Drive around. The occasional acid flashback."
Jeff Bridges as the world's coolest bowler in The Big Lebowski.

CURVE BALLS

Ten pin bowling balls are technical bits of kit. Factors to be taken into account in their manufacture include the ball's radius of gyration, coefficient of restitution, surface hardness and hooking potential. No we don't know either, but this may explain why they cost up to £150 or more.

King Henry VIII used cannon balls for bowling.

There are two different types of bowling grips: conventional, and finger tip. In a conventional grip, the bowler's ring and middle fingers are placed into the ball up to the second joint; in a finger tip grip the ring and middle fingers are inserted into the ball up to the first joint. More strength is needed for the finger tip grip but it gives the bowler better control in rotating the ball.

VITAL STATISTICS

Diameter: 8.5-8.595ins (21.6-21.8cm).

Weight: 16lbs (7.3kg) or less. No minimum weight is specified.

One of over 100 million regular ten-pin bowlers, thinking 'ARSE': Angle, Release, Speed, Equipment . . .

THE BOWLING BALL

There is evidence dating back to 3200 BC of games in ancient Egypt which involved rolling a ball along a flat surface to knock down skittles. Later evidence shows bowling games in Dark Ages Germany, but the first written record comes from 1366 when King Edward III banned bowling in England (see also football, lawn bowls, cricket etc. – this guy was a real killjoy) so that people could concentrate on firing arrows at the French.

During the same period a game called Kegel was developed in Germany which involved bowling at nine skittles. This, along with English and Dutch versions of bowling, was introduced to America during the colonial era, and there is evidence of a ten-pin game being played in Britain in the early 19th century.

Nine-pin bowling in the USA was eventually banned in 1841 because of its links with organised gambling – so ten-pin bowling was 'invented' to get around the ban. By this time the first indoor bowling alley had opened in New York, using balls made from a heavy wood known as lignum vitae, which is so dense it will sink in water. However, in 1905 the first rubber bowling ball was produced, whilst in 1914 Brunswick began to manufacture balls made from Mineralite, a hard rubber compound.

This remained the standard compound for bowling balls until the 1970s, when polyester was introduced, although early polyester balls sometimes became lopsided depending on the treatments they underwent in manufacture. This was followed by Ebonite's first polyurethane ball in 1981, which had a better grip on wooden lane surfaces. In the early 1990s Nu-Line developed the reactive resin surface which is common on modern balls, since when developments in bowling balls have been so rapid that it's been almost impossible for the rules of the game to keep up.

In particular the design of the ball's core underwent huge changes. Prior to the 90s it had basically been a heavy sphere inside the ball; after about 1990 all manner of computer designed core shapes were introduced for different weights of ball, with a phenomenally fast turnover in designs, whilst additional weights and counter-weights were also added to the core or placed elsewhere inside the ball.

The core essentially affects the way the ball rolls when bowled, and is an attempt to stabilise it. Cores consist of various materials including dense plastic, ceramics or a resin/graphite mix, whilst iron oxide or the exotic sounding zirconium (from the Planet Zog) may be used for counterweights.

The net effect of all this is that 'perfect games' (12 successive throws in which all 10 pins are knocked over) have become increasingly common, leading to the not unjustified argument that using modern balls requires less skill from the bowler, and the introduction of 'dynamic balance' regulations which require a PhD in physics to understand.

The three finger holes also affect the behaviour of the ball since they affect the core dynamics. They are drilled into the ball after manufacture to suit the bowler's hand, with a hole for the thumb, ring and middle finger, although up to five holes are allowed (and there are other forms of bowling called five-pin and candlepin which use smaller balls and thus don't require finger holes). Customised balls may allow the bowler to bowl with a ball a pound or two heavier than a non-customised model.

Technology has also allowed balls to become increasingly flamboyant in design, with surfaces featuring everything from multiple and iridescent colours to designs that appear to have objects embedded within the ball.

However, despite all this the ball still has to be bowled with some modicum of skill if it's to achieve the desired aim of knocking over as many pins as possible. This doesn't just depend on skill with the ball and the type of ball used however – the bowling lane has a huge effect too. For instance, wooden bowling lanes are 'oiled' on a regular basis, with the first two-thirds receiving the heaviest application of oil, which results in the ball sliding (as opposed to rolling) down the top two-thirds of the lane, then spinning and curving when it hits the drier, less well-oiled end. All this, plus the way the ball rotates and the effect of individual delivery style is taken into account by top players.

Major manufacturers today include AMF, Brunswick Corporation and Ebonite International, all of whom have been involved with ten-pin bowling from its early days. The worldwide market is estimated at over 100 million people, making ten-pin bowling (along with several other games) the 'world's most popular sport' after football.

BOWLING SLANG

Action - The amount of spin placed on a ball. A slower ball with more action can be more effective at disrupting the pins than a faster ball with less action.

Address - The stance a player takes before beginning the approach.

ARSE - An acronym describing the four basic adjustments used by players to establish their optimum strike line. Angle, Release, Speed, Equipment.

Big Ears - A difficult split in which the remaining four pins are split between the two sides of the lane.

Boomer - A ball with a very large hook.

Cranker - A shot of immense speed and power with a very aggressive hook in the back-end.

Dump - A ball released into the air that lands on the lane loudly.

Gutter Ball - A ball that travels into the gutter before reaching the pins.

Head Pin - The 1-pin, the closest pin to the foul line.

Inside Line - A roll that starts from near the centre of the lane (third, fourth or fifth arrows), instead of the outside edge.

Leave - The pins left after the first ball of a frame has been rolled.

Loafing - Delivering the ball onto the lane without enough lift.

Morph - A pin that moves across the deck without falling over.

Naked Spare - A single pin spare leave.

Pocket - The optimum point for the ball to hit the pins generally just behind the front pin.

Poison Ivy - A difficult split which leaves three pins, two on one side of the lane, one on the other.

Railroad - A wide split between two pins, with both occupying the same line.

Rock - A slang term for the bowling ball. The ball is also sometimes referred to as an 'apple'.

Split - A pin formation in which some pins including the head pin have been knocked down on the first roll in a frame.

Stroker - A delivery that aims more for accuracy than a cranker.

Strike - The process of knocking all the pins down using only the first roll in a frame.

Turkey - Three strikes in a row.

Turkey buzzard - Three splits in a row.

ON THE BALL

"I wasn't going for any big ones today."
Eighteen-year-old Venus Williams after a record breaking serve of over 125mph.

Andre Agassi to Andy Roddick: "Let's see what you've got, big boy."
Roddick to Agassi: "Hair."

"I love Wimbledon. But why don't they stage it in the summer?"
Indian legend Vijay Amritraj during the sodden 2007 Wimbledon Championships.

CURVE BALLS

No-one is quite sure where the name Tennis comes from. Two possible origins are from the French word 'tenez', which means 'take it/take that,' which may have been shouted upon serving the ball; the other, far more speculative theory is that it originated in an Egyptian town called Tinnis on the banks of the Nile.

The service was apparently invented by Henry VIII, who had servants throw the ball up for him to strike as he was too fat to do it himself (kind of makes you wonder how he got himself around the court . . .).

There is some debate over who has the fastest serve. Records include those of 'Big Bill' Tilden (USA) at 163.6mph way back in 1931 and Mike Sangster (GB) at 154mph in 1963, whilst Venus Williams (USA) holds the women's record at 127.4mph. That said a German tennis coach and statistician, Horst Goepper, claimed a serving speed of 199.53 mph under test conditions in 1981.

About 42,000 balls are used at the Wimbledon Championship.

VITAL STATISTICS

International Tennis Federation rules state the following:

Diameter: More than 2½ins, but less than 2 5/8 ins.

Weight: More than 2oz, but less than 2 1/16oz.

When dropped onto a concrete base from 100 inches, the ball should bounce more than 53 inches, but less than 58 inches.

The 'stiffness' of the balls, defined by how much they deform (curve in or out) under 18lbs of pressure, must be more than .220ins and less than .290ins for forward deformation.

For return deformation it must be more than .315ins and less than .425ins.

The rules do not say what material the cover should be made from, its thickness, or how tightly or loosely the fibres are woven.

Balls are usually pressurised to about 12lb/sq.in.

THE TENNIS BALL

Tennis almost certainly derived from the simple pleasure of two people knocking a ball back and forth with the palms of their hands, and there is evidence of this dating back thousands of years to the ancient Egyptians, Greeks and Romans. Some believe it developed from the Roman game of **harpastum**, which interestingly is also regarded by some as a precursor to football, rugby and quite a few other ball games.

However, it's from medieval France that the first accounts of a game approximating to modern tennis originate, with records of 11th century monks knocking a crudely-fashioned ball back and forth by hand over a rope stretched across, for example, the monastery quadrangle (which if you think about it vaguely resembles a modern tennis court – except for the presence of robed monks …) At this time it was known as 'jeu de palme' due to the use of the palms. Around the 12th century leather gloves were introduced to protect the hand, but it was not until the 16th century that short bats were introduced and the game began to look more like tennis as we know it today. Kind of …

It's not surprising that a glove, then a racquet, were eventually used for thwacking the ball around since early tennis balls were made from leather stuffed with wool or horse hair and were hard on the palm of the hand when hit continuously.

Things became a little more high tech in the 18th century when thin strips of wool were wound tightly around an inner core which was then tied up with string, and the whole lot would then be stitched inside a white cloth outer.

However, at this stage we're talking about Real Tennis, an indoor court game that was popular amongst both French and British medieval royalty (hence the term 'court' for the playing area). The name 'real' is considered by some to derive from 'royal' because of this, but see p196 for the 'real' explanation). The game's popularity declined in the 17th century, however, and outdoor tennis didn't come into being until the late 19th century in two parallel developments in the UK.

In 1872 the world's first tennis club was formed in Leamington Spa, based on a game developed by Major Harry Gem and Augurio Pereira which combined elements of rackets and pelota (see p194). Then the following year the splendidly-monikored Major Walter Clopton Wingfield designed a very similar game with the somewhat pretentious name of **Sphairistike** (from (Greek σφάιρίστική, 'skill at playing at ball'), based on real tennis and using much of the French terminology of the original sport. It took only four more years before the first Wimbledon championships were held.

Tennis balls at this time were already quite technical in design, initially using a solid India rubber sphere, although it was soon found that they lasted longer and were better to play with if flannel was stitched on top of the rubber inner.

A solid ball wasn't used for long – instead a hollow rubber sphere was introduced, which was cut to shape using 'clover leaf' segments joined together and assembled by a special machine designed for the purpose, but not before being filled with pressurising gases which were 'activated' as the core was moulded by heat into a spherical shape. This was then covered in flannel – Victorian ingenuity at its finest.

The flannel was eventually replaced by hard wearing 'Melton' cloth, a tight woven woollen cloth which originated in Melton Mowbray and is also used in donkey jackets. This is still used today, along with needle cloth, which is less hard wearing.

As the game developed, it reached levels of skill where a more predictable ball construction was needed, which saw the introduction of two separate rubber hemispheres joined together either under pressure or using a more complicated chemical decomposition process to form internal pressure.

The fabric on a modern tennis ball is first woven using cotton as a backing (warp) and a wool/nylon mix for the covering (weft), after which it's dyed and finished, then two 'dogbones' of fabric are cut after application of a latex backing and stuck to the latex-covered core, with what was once stitching now replaced by a vulcanised rubber seam. The ball is then cured and tumbled slowly through a steam-laden atmosphere, which causes the cloth to fluff, giving a raised and softer surface, whilst the ridge where the two halves of the ball are cemented together also disappears.

Logos are then applied before the balls are packed in pressurised cans to preserve their internal pressure. Pressurised balls will lose their pressure about a month after

FEELING FUZZY

The 'fuzzy' surface of the felt outer is a vital component in how tennis balls travel through the air and allow players to impart spin to the ball, since it creates air drag and friction which allows backspin, topspin etc. Scientific papers have been written on this, the ITF have tested tennis balls in wind tunnels and even NASA has studied their aerodynamics.

As Dr Rabi Mehta, a world authority on sports ball aerodynamics says, "Fuzz drag makes the aerodynamics of the tennis ball even more interesting since the fuzz elements change orientation with increased velocity and the fuzz wears off during play."

Or for the scientifically minded, you can calculate your tennis ball's drag coefficient (Co) and Reynolds number (Re), which describes the speed of a sphere, by the simple application of the following:

$Co = D/0.5 \, q \, u2 \, A$

Where D is the drag force, q is the density of air, 1.21 kg/m2, u is the velocity of the ball relative to the fluid, and A the cross-sectional area.

And $Re = q \, d \, u \, / \, g$
Where d is the ball diameter and g the viscosity of the fluid, 1.81E-5 Poise for air. (John Dunlop, Acousto-Scan, Aug 03).

Simple – why not do it in the comfort of your own home . . .?

the can is opened. However, not all tennis balls are pressurised. You can also buy pressureless balls with a solid core, which are used mainly for training. They don't lose their bounce like pressurised balls, although the felt will wear off eventually.

Older readers will recall the Technicolor splendour that was the introduction of yellow balls by the International Tennis Federation in 1972 (or in the case of Wimbledon, ever the trend setters, 1986). These were found to be more visible to TV viewers, since until then tennis balls were white (or occasionally black depending on the background colour of the court). Until 1989 there was only one type of tennis ball used officially in competition play. Then 'high altitude' balls were introduced to allow for different atmospheric pressure at altitude. In 2002, 'Type 1' and 'Type 3' balls were introduced, with the majority of balls used in play – whether competition or recreation – being 'Type 2'.

The majority of tennis balls are made in the Far East for the usual reasons – cheaper labour and raw materials, and fewer health and safety and union issues. Tennis balls will vary slightly by manufacturer and model, and experienced players can instantly tell the difference between balls – they may feel lighter or heavier, harder or softer, more or less bouncy, have a coarser or finer cover and require varying degrees of effort in order to generate the same speed.

Pete Sampras figures out
$C_0 = D/0.5 \, q \, u^2 \, A$ once again.

ON THE BALL

"I always suspected it was a ridiculous sport, but not until the [2008 Olympic] Games did I learn the rules state there is a maximum size for the bikinis worn by the female players. A sport for the dirty old men Olympics, not the proper Olympics."
Lawrence Donegan, Guardian correspondent, gets humourlessly PC in a typically PC-type way.

". . . we wear a bikini because it is hot out there most of the time."
Aussie beach volleyball star Natalie Cooke sets Mr. Donegan straight (although one could feasibly ask why the men don't wear them too in that case . . .).

CURVE BALLS

Indian female beach volleyball players (unlike Natalie Cooke) refused to wear bikinis in the 2008 World Beach Volleyball tournament because they deemed them 'objectionable'.

The longest recorded volleyball marathon by two teams of six is 75 hours 30 minutes at Kingston, North Carolina in 1980.

Most volleyball players jump about 300 times a match.

On a global basis, volleyball ranks only behind football in 'participation sports' (what other sort of sport is there?) with over 800 million players worldwide. This makes it at least the fourth sport in this book to claim to be the second most popular in the world.

VITAL STATISTICS

Material: A rubber bladder covered with leather or canvas.

Circumference: 25.5–26.5ins/65–67cm.
(beach volleyball 26–27 ins/66–68cm)

Weight: Between 9.2–9.9oz/260-280g.
(beach volleyball the same)

Internal pressure: 4.3–4.6psi/0.3–0.325kgf/cm2.
(beach volleyball 2.5–3.2psi/0.175–0.225kgf/cm2.

THE VOLLEYBALL BALL

Of all the planet's major ball sports, volleyball is the only one that could be said to be truly American. Its forerunner, a game known as Mintonette, was invented on 9 February 1895 in Holyoke, Massachusetts by one William G. Morgan, a YMCA physical education director. As it happens this corner of the USA could justifiably lay claim to being the birthplace of much of American sport, since Basketball was invented four years earlier by Canadian James Naismith just ten miles away, and American Football and Baseball saw much of their early development taking place in this part of the country.

Morgan was looking to develop an alternative to Basketball which involved less physical contact for older YMCA members, and took component parts of handball (hitting the ball) and tennis (the net) to make up his new game. "In search of an appropriate game, tennis occurred to me, but this required rackets, balls, a net and other equipment, so it was eliminated – but the idea of a net seemed a good one," he said. "We raised it to a height of about 6 feet 6 inches (1.98m) from the ground, just above the head of an average man. We needed a ball, and among those we tried was a Basketball bladder, but this was too light and too slow, we therefore tried the Basketball itself, which was too big and too heavy."

Cue another familiar figure in late 19th century US sports – A.G. Spalding Esq. Spalding's company was already manufacturing basketballs, American footballs and baseballs for the burgeoning US market and now picked up another contract to make a ball specifically for what was eventually to become known as volleyball (the name was suggested – and subsequently adopted – at an exhibition match in 1896 by Alfred Halstead).

The leather sphere Spalding came up with had a rubber bladder and was the same size and weight as a modern volleyball. From there the uptake and growth of the sport were phenomenal. After a few tweaks to the rules by the International YMCA Training School it had already reached Japan and Asia by the end of 1896 thanks to the YMCA's international network and soon became tremendously popular in its native country.

Some 200,000 people were playing the sport in the USA by 1916, and a further surge in popularity came at the end of WW1 when around 16,000 volleyballs were distributed to US troops and their allies (no doubt to the great delight of Spalding) by the American Expeditionary Force as they turned up late for the war in 1919.

As with so many other major sports the French shouldered their way into Volleyball in 1947 with the formation of an international governing body, the Fédération International de Volleyball (FIVB), whilst Beach Volleyball, which originated on the sunny beaches of California in the 1920s, had to wait until 1987 to be offered its own world championships by the FIVB.

As far as the actual ball is concerned, unlike many sports there have been no changes to the dimensions since the earliest days of the game, and the design has remained much the same, consisting of eighteen rectangular panels of leather or synthetic material wrapped around a bladder, with a valve to regulate internal air pressure. The panels are arranged in six identical sections of three panels each.

Beach volleyballs are slightly larger than regular volleyballs and have a rougher surface. Also, despite weighing the same, they have a lower internal pressure which makes them softer. Naturally enough in such a flamboyant sport, they tend to be very brightly coloured in comparison to their regular brethren.

Spalding's grip on the volleyball market was broken long ago by several other manufacturers, particularly those from Japan. In 1952, Tachikara produced a revolutionary seamless ball – more commonly referred to these days as a moulded or laminated ball – in place of traditional asymmetrical hand-stitched balls. This improved the ball's spherical shape, air retention, rebound, and overall durability.

Later developments by the company included its patented if strange-sounding Loose Bladder Construction (LBC) method, which allows a layer of air to circulate between the inside bladder and a cotton canvas/leather outside cover, resulting in a truer flight and a superior soft touch. The company's seamless LBC volleyball was introduced at the 1964 Olympic Games in Tokyo, when Volleyball itself made its Olympic debut (Beach Volleyball had to wait until 1992 to appear at the Olympics).

A further development by the company was their Dual Bladder Construction (DBC) volleyball in 2003, featuring two internal, independent bladders with an impact-reducing layer of air circulating between the two, resulting in a ball that is theoretically twice as durable and responsive with improved control and flight.

Mikasa, a company whose Japanese origins date back to 1917, saw things take off after setting up shop in California in the 1970s, so much so that by 2008 their eight-panelled dimpled ball had been adopted by the FIVB and the Beijing Olympics as the official indoor ball on account of its greater accuracy, better feel, truer flight and softer touch, whilst their VLS200 'Beach Champ' ball was also used in the Olympic beach volleyball competition.

Another major manufacturer is **Molten**, also Japanese. Their volleyballs are made from an outer layer of micro-fibre based synthetic leather which is as soft as a natural leather ball and also absorbs perspiration as well as genuine leather, but retains a dry surface better than natural leather. Inside this is a rubber cover which helps to improve durability and creates a better feel, and this in turn contains a butyl or latex bladder. Butyl bladders have extremely low air-permeability, which helps to retain internal pressure throughout a game and are best used on hard surfaces, whilst latex bladders are softer and have greater air permeability, making them better for use on softer surfaces, although they need to be inflated before use.

The worldwide success of volleyball is obvious and whilst most Americans would be surprised and disappointed to discover that none of the traditional American sports have truly American origins, here's one sport they did invent that they can be proud of. Particularly ladies' Beach Volleyball, Mr. Donegan.

800 million players worldwide can't be wrong. Volleyball is the planet's second biggest sport. Along with four or five others . . .

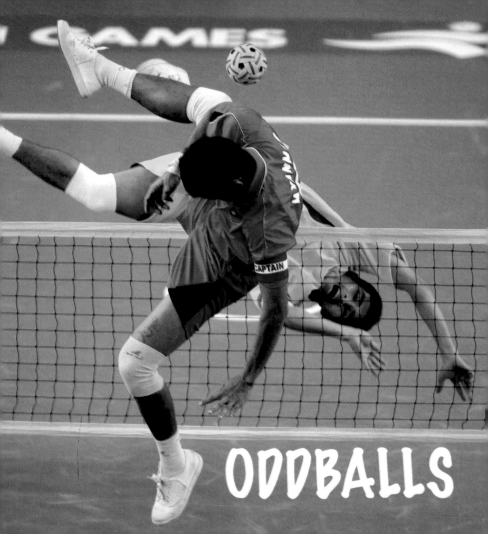

ODDBALLS

ODDBALLS

If you play any of the sports listed in this final chapter you may well take offence at their inclusion in the 'Oddballs' bin. The fact remains, however, that on a global scale most of the sports mentioned here, with the possible exception of Netball, are practised by lesser numbers and in fewer countries than those enjoying the privilege of a chapter to themselves.

But hey, what of it? A bit of individuality is what sport is all about . . .

ON THE BALL
"The stopwatch has stopped. It's up to God and the referee now. The referee is Pat Horan. God is God."
Legendary commentator Micheal O'Muircheartaigh with some incisive observations during a tense Gaelic football match.

AUSSIE RULES FOOTBALL

Aussie Rules is also known as 'footy', 'football' and 'AFL', thus creating even more confusion amongst non-believers. The best balls are generally considered to be made by the companies Sherrin and Burley, with Sherrin's models being manufactured from cowhide and stitched by machine. Cheaper synthetic rubber models are also available, usually Chinese imports, and good on the Aussies, you can also buy a Fair Trade Aussie Rules ball made in Pakistan.

Essentially a 'prolate sphere' like a rugby ball, an Aussie Rules ball looks much the same as said rugby ball, but it's slightly smaller and more rounded with raised stitching on the main seam.

T.W. Sherrin made the first ball specifically designed for Aussie Rules, which came about after he was given a rugby ball to fix in 1880. The game had been played for several years prior to this as a means of keeping cricketers fit in the off-season. Its origins date back to the 1850s when various forms of 'foot-ball' were played in different parts of Oz, with the rules developed in Melbourne in 1858 becoming dominant.

This was largely at the instigation of one Tom Wills, who was influenced by rugby union after being schooled in England, although these early games were played with a round ball and had up to 40 players per side.

Long the most popular ball game in Australia, especially in the states of South Australia and Victoria, that's pretty much where it ends – Oz is the only country with a professional league and although there are amateur leagues in around 50 other countries it's never really taken off abroad.

CURVE BALL
An Aboriginal ball game called **Marn Grook** may well have had an influence on Aussie Rules since the 'mark' in Aussie Rules – leaping to catch a high ball – was a feature of the game.

Strewth! Aussie rules
is a man's game.

BANDY

Bandy is essentially a form of ice hockey using a ball instead of a puck. Unlike ice hockey, handling of the ball is not allowed and it's generally less violent. The ball was originally a cork or other square wooden block, which then developed into a rounded piece of cork with a knitted and painted outer layer. Modern bandy balls are made of plastic and just under an inch in diameter.

The game has been played throughout northern Europe since the Middle Ages and is now mainly played in Scandinavia, Russia, Canada and the USA although it was once popular in England, especially on the frozen ponds of the Fens – in fact England were European Champions in 1913. A similar game called Bando was also played in Wales in the 16th century, particularly around the Vale of Glamorgan. Bandy will be trialled at the 2010 Winter Olympics in Vancouver.

ON THE BALL
"It's a much faster, more exciting game than indoor ice hockey."
Bob Burn-Murdoch, curator of The Norris Museum in St Ives, Norfolk, bigs up Bandy.

DODGEBALL

As the film of the same name, released in 2004 and starring Ben Stiller, showed, Dodgeball is a team sport in which the main objective of each team of 4 to 10 players is to eliminate all members of the opposing team by hitting them with thrown balls, catching a ball thrown by a member of the opposing team, or forcing them to move outside the court boundaries when a ball is thrown at them.

Unlike most ball sports more than one ball is used in a game. Usually each team has six balls (but in larger games can be up to 10) to hurl at their opponents, which are placed on the centreline before the referee blows the whistle to start the game. Then the madness commences.

There is no standard size or material for the ball. Any old ball will do. The most common is volleyball-sized and made of foam with a plastic outer shell.

Dodgeball is also one of the few games in which eliminated players can return to play. If a player catches a ball thrown by an opponent they can either eliminate that player, or bring back the last player from their own team to leave the field of play.

For a minority sport, it's not only had its own feature film, but also featured on episodes of *South Park*, *The Simpsons* and *Freaks and Geeks*.

CURVE BALL

Ben Stiller was nominated for Worst Actor in the 25th annual Golden Raspberry Awards for his role as White Goodman in *Dodgeball*.

Dodgeball is one of Japan's biggest elementary school sports.

FLOORBALL

Popular in northern Europe and Scandinavia, Floorball was developed in Sweden in the 1970s and is a little like indoor hockey in that it uses a stick and ball. However, the ball is very different to that used in hockey, being made of lightweight plastic (standard weight 23g, diameter 72mm) and with 26 holes, each 11mm in diameter. The ball's holey surface may be either smooth or dimpled, with 1,500 or more dimples on a precision ball. The dimples reduce air resistance and friction making for a faster, if harder, ball to control.

At around only €2 a pop, floorballs are one of the cheapest balls of any ball sport and come in a range of colours as well as glow-in-the-dark flavour. In its home country of Sweden the sport is called Innebandy or 'indoor bandy' after the game it is most closely related to.

GAELIC FOOTBALL

One of the world's oldest sports, Gaelic Football at first glance appears to be played with a soccer ball, but in fact the ball is heavier – the official dimensions are weight: 450g–480g and circumference: 68cm–70cm. It has a leather panelled surface with horizontal stitching of the panels like older style soccer balls or modern volleyballs.

One of Ireland's most popular games, Gaelic football has been played on the Emerald Isle since at least the 12th century, which is when the first written record of it appears. Being Ireland it was suitably controversial, with a player called William Bernard being 'accidentally stabbed' by a spectator, John McCrocan, in a game at Newcastle, County Dublin.

Never a game for the weak and feeble, early matches roamed over entire parishes and lasted a whole day, with wrestling, holding and tripping allowed. As a catching, kicking and running game, there are many similarities between Gaelic football and

Aussie rules, and frequently acrimonious games of a mix of the two sports called 'international rules football' are held between the two countries.

ON THE BALL

"Australians are deeply unpleasant when they lose and unbearable when they win." *Jerome O'Reilly of Ireland's* Sunday Independent *observes a fact that Englishmen have long known after a strife-ridden 'international rules football' game between Ireland and Australia in 2006.*

CURVE BALL

On Bloody Sunday in 1920 a Gaelic football match at Croke Park in Dublin was raided by British forces during which 14 people were killed and 65 injured.

JORKYBALL

Yet to celebrate its quarter century, Jorkyball® was invented in 1987 by Frenchman Gilles Paniez in a garage in Lyon, and is a bit like soccer meets squash. Using a handsewn 32-panel felt ball weighing 200g and with a diameter of 48.5cm, it involves two players on each side kicking a ball around inside a 10m x 5m 'cage' with a 'pitch' of artificial turf and the option to use the walls as in squash.

The name of the game is a registered trademark and inventor Paniez is now president of the Fédération Internationale des Associations 2x2 Jorkyball® and of the opinion that jorkyball®, "... has all the characteristics of a sport ... which may explode".

Sounds interesting . . .

CURVE BALL

The 'pitch' used for Jorkyball® goes by the marvellous geometric name of a parallele-piped, which as we all know is a three-dimensional figure formed by six parallelograms. And a parallelipiped is, of course, a subclass of the prismatoids . . .

KNUR AND SPELL

As a Yorkshireman I'm duty bound to mention the somewhat arcane Yorkshire pastime of Knur and Spell. The game dates back to at least the 1300s, achieved world domination in the 1970s when it featured regularly on Yorkshire Television (and as everyone knows the 'world' for a Yorkshireman is that area within the borders of God's own county), but has subsequently all but died out. A very similar game called Nipsy is also played in South Yorkshire.

The knur/nipsy is a small round ball about the same size as a billiard ball, which is placed in a cup on a spring – the spell. When the spell is touched by a 'trip stick', the knur flies into the air and the player attempts to whack it as far as possible with said trip stick.

The knur is ceramic, whilst a nipsy can be made from lignum vitae or Permali, a wood/resin substitute. Knur and Spell requires a longer pitch than nipsy, the latter of which can be played on a football pitch – lack of appropriate space probably being one reason for Knur and Spell's decline. That said, it can still be seen at the following Yorkshire pubs, all of which I can personally recommend: The Robin Hood, Mytholmroyd; The Spring Rock, Upper Barkisland; The Sportsman Inn, Midgley and The Tempest Arms, Elsack.

ON THE BALL
"Ah'll sithee."
Presenter Fred Trueman's standard 'goodbye' at the end of Yorkshire Television's much-lamented 70s programme, Indoor League, *which featured beer drinking, chain smoking northern 'sportsmen' excelling at such practices as Knur and Spell and arm wrestling.*

CURVE BALL
Former world Knur and Spell champion Frank Lenthall hit a knur 3 chains 6 yards and 2 feet at Elland, West Yorkshire in the 1970s. That's almost 293 yards in new money.

KORFBALL

Korfball is perhaps unique in that it is played by two mixed teams of eight with four men and four women on each side. Very similar to Basketball and Netball, and played with a ball very similar to a soccer ball, it was invented in the Netherlands in 1901 (just ten years after Basketball) by Amsterdam schoolmaster Nico Broekhuysen, who wanted a game that girls and boys could play together as equals. Some may call him delusional, but Korfball has had a reasonable measure of success, having regular world championships and being played in around 50 countries, with indoor, outdoor and beach options.

The basic aim of Korfball is to score by getting the ball into a basket (the korf – Dutch for basket) which is open at both ends with its rim 3.5m above the ground, but which has no basketball-style backboard.

The technical details for a korfball are circumference: 68–70.5cm, weight: 445–475g (which is slightly bigger and heavier than a soccer ball) and when dropped from a height of 1.80m it should rebound to between 1.10–1.30m. In addition it should be two colours, generally black and white, and it usually comes with a diagonal pattern and is made from leather or synthetic leather. The major manufacturer of korfballs is the Japanese company Mikasa.

The symmetrical pattern on the ball helps to prevent players from losing the visual effect of the ball being round in shape when it's in play. This presumably applies to all balls, although it took research on korfball to glean this vital nugget of information.

Dutch schoolchildren attempt to score in the korf.

LACROSSE

Lacrosse is the oldest team sport in North America, if you can call a game played by up to 1,000 men over three days on a pitch as long as two miles a 'team sport' rather than an organised riot.

This was the way Native Americans played it anyway, as a celebration of their spiritual life and world, using a rudimentary ball made from anything from stone and clay to wood, knotted leather strips, or hair-stuffed deerskin. European settlers took to the game (which is thought to have derived from the French term for field hockey, 'la jeu de la crosse') and tidied up the 'rules' somewhat so that by 1867 Lacrosse had been codified by the founder of Montreal Lacrosse Club, Dr William George Beers.

An indoor version of the game was introduced in the 1930s called Box Lacrosse, and whilst Lacrosse has remained a minority sport elsewhere in the world, in the USA and Canada both the indoor and outdoor versions have become major draws, so much so that Lacrosse is now Canada's official 'National Summer Sport' – a bit like cricket for the English (except the Canadians still know how to play their national game).

Modern Lacrosse balls are solid rubber spheres, usually white, although a wide range of other colours may be used, with a circumference of 7.75-8ins (19-20cm) and a weight of 5-5.25 ounces (140-150g). Major manufacturers are the American companies Brine and Warrior, the latter of which in 2002 introduced the orange 'grippy' ball to Major League Lacrosse to help fans follow the game both live and on TV. This new ball is textured, making it less weather sensitive and giving a better feel for the player   carrying it in the stick pocket.

ON THE BALL
"I thought Lacrosse was what you find in la church."
Comedian Robin Williams, witty as ever.

CURVE BALL
At the end of a Lacrosse game the winning team gets to keep the ball.

MARBLES

Whether marbles are toys or sports gear is a moot point, but there's no doubt that they are the most attractive and varied of all balls. 'Sporting' marbles can vary in size from ¼ inch (0.635cm) to over 3ins (7.75cm) in diameter, and may be made from glass, clay or agate. But those used in competitions such as the World Championships must be 15.5mm in diameter, although they can be made from any non-metal material.

There are wide variations in marbles games, which are played acros the globe, and there's even a Marbles World Championship. Being a relatively simple item to produce, it's no surprise that hand-made marbles of stone, small rocks, clay, minerals, steel, glass or, indeed, marble have been found in societies worldwide, dating back as far as the ancient Egyptians. They became hugely popular in England in the Victorian era. Mass-produced ceramic marbles have been around since the 1870s and mass-produced glass marbles since the early 20th century. These are the most popular, purely for aesthetic reasons and have their various swirls of colour added as the glass cools.

CURVE BALL
Marbles players particularly value 'sunnies,' which are made of coloured glass, are semi-transparent and contain small air bubbles within the glass. It's supposedly possible (although not recommended) to observe a solar eclipse through a 'sunny' without suffering eye damage, hence the name.

Marbles: every schoolboy's dream playground game.

NETBALL

Despite its image as a thoroughly spiffing game for hearty English schoolgirls, Netball was, in fact, invented in the USA in 1895 as 'basketball for women'. Indeed, inventor Clara Gregory Baer, of the University of Louisiana, actually asked for advice from Basketball inventor James Naismith (see p26) prior to coming up with the rules for the sport.

Within a year Netball was being played in England and quickly spread to the colonies, proving especially popular in the West Indies, Australia and New Zealand, although surprisingly it has only been played at the Commonwealth Games since 1998, despite being recognised as an Olympic sport three years earlier.

Being a relatively new game with distinct rules from its inception there have been few changes to the ball since the early days, when basketballs were initially used to play. Modern netballs are essentially lighter, smaller and a little softer than a modern basketball, with the same construction techniques. That said, a netball looks much more like a volleyball, with panels, made from grippable surface materials such as rubber, leather or synthetics, either stitched or engraved onto the surface. The colour is usually white, with added graphics to liven things up a bit.

One of the major manufacturers is Gilbert, whose top of the line 'Xact-7' ball uses a multi-laminate panel construction with a butyl bladder and a top grade natural rubber surface with specifically designed pimples for better grip and accuracy.

Standard weight is 400-450g; circumference 690-710mm.

ON THE BALL
"I didn't like netball – I used to get wolf whistles because of my short skirts."
Princess Anne. Yes, hard to believe, but then toffs live in a different world to the rest of us.

PELOTA

Pelota is a Spanish word for a variety of court games played with hand/bat/basket and ball which originated in the Basque country (Basque and Catalan: 'pilota'; French: 'pelote'). It is said to derive from the French game of Real Tennis.

There are various forms of the game on different-sized courts, and the type of ball used depends on the type of game. In the version where the palm of the hand is used the ball weighs between 92-95g and is traditionally made of wool wrapped around a solid core – regular players usually end up with a 'swollen' hand as a result of the impacts.

Those varieties involving bats (wooden) use either a rubber or leather ball, while the basket game (known as Cesta Punta in Spanish and Jai Alai in the USA) sees players utilising a 'glove' which extends into a long basket in which a rubber ball is caught and hurled back at the court wall in a similar fashion to squash.

As with so many other sports, proponents of Cesta Punta claim that it is the world's fastest ball game, and they may have a point. In 1979 José Ramón Areitio unleashed a ball at a speed of 302kmph in a game in Rhode Island, USA.

CURVE BALL
Pelota has featured four times at the Olympics – as an official sport in Paris (1900) and as a demonstration sport at the games of 1924 (Paris), 1968 (Mexico) and 1992 (Barcelona).

Even though Pelota is one of the fastest ball sports in the world, with the ball reaching speeds of up to 302kmph, some games are played with a flaming ball to add 'intensity'.

POLO

Despite my best efforts I was unable to find authenticated accounts of human heads and small animals being used as the 'ball' in early games of Polo, which let's face it for most members of the hoi polloi is all that really interests us about a game that is so stratospherically beyond our means as to be totally inconsequential.

Be that as it may, Polo has a history dating back to ancient Persia some 2,000 years ago and, whilst it's mainly been a game restricted to royalty and aristocrats, in some instances mere commoners were allowed to join in astride their fleabitten ponies.

Polo had spread to India by the 16th century, where it became popular amongst officers of the British Raj with fine upstanding names like Edward 'Chicken' Hartopp (of the 10th Hussars, by Jove!), who brought it back to Blighty. The first Polo club in Britain was formed in Monmouthshire in 1872 by a sterling cove named Captain Francis 'Tip' Herbert (of the 7th Lancers – huzzah!). And true to form, the Brits then took it to the rest of the world, which subsequently went on to show them how it should be played etc.

The name derives from the Tibetan word for ball – pulu – which in the early days of the game was made from the roots of bamboo or willow. Modern polo balls are made from an inflated leather-covered sphere about 4.5ins (11.4cm) in diameter (for indoor games) and 3¼ins (8.3cm) for outdoor games, with a weight of around 4oz (113.4g). Not that you're ever likely to need to buy one, like . . .

ON THE BALL
"Playing Polo is like trying to play golf during an earthquake."
Sylvester Stallone.

CURVE BALL
People seem to like hitting balls with a stick whilst astraddle something – varieties of polo include canoe, cycle, camel, elephant, golfcart, Segway (one of those two-wheeled electronic cart things), BMX and winter. My favourite, however, has to be Yak Polo.

REAL TENNIS

Real Tennis' origins are, unsurprisingly, closely linked to lawn tennis, with the medieval French game of jeu de palme generally being regarded their joint forerunner. The idea that the 'real' was a derivation of 'royal' is wrong – it was simply a way of differentiating it from the later game of 'lawn tennis.'

Real Tennis was massive in Europe in the 16th and 17th century, with Henry VIII being a major patron and player and Charles IX of France creating a 'professional tour' in 1571. This was the golden era for the sport, however, and only a handful of Real Tennis courts remain in Europe, the USA and Australia today.

At first glance the ball looks quite similar to a 'regular' tennis ball, with the same design and colour (white or 'optic yellow') but it's actually larger and heavier (diameter 2½ ins/64mm; weight 2½oz/71g) and considerably less bouncy. Real Tennis balls are handmade, with a cork core which is tightly wound with fabric tape then covered in a hand-sewn layer of hard-wearing, woollen Melton or Needle cloth, as are lawn tennis balls. This extra weight and lack of bounce make spin an integral part of the game for any good Real Tennis player.

ON THE BALL
"We will, in France, by God's grace, play a set [that] shall strike his father's crown into the hazard . . . And tell the pleasant Prince this mock of his hath turn'd his balls to gun stones."
King Henry after receiving a set of Real Tennis balls in mockery from the French Dauphin, Henry V, Act I – Scene II.

CURVE BALL
Two French kings died from Real Tennis-related episodes – hurrah! Sorry . . . Louis X expired after contracting a cold whilst playing, and Charles VIII met his maker after being struck by a ball.

ROUNDERS

Rounders is the English school-based game, mainly for girls, from which Baseball grew. But, in fact, Rounders itself may be derived from the game of stoolball (see p199). The ball used in rounders varies depending on which of the sport's strongholds the game is played in. In England the ball used in school games, which make up the majority of Rounders matches, is often just a tennis ball, whilst for more serious games a hard ball with a cork core and a white leather outer with raised red stitching will be used. The exact circumference should be 190mm (7.5ins). In Ireland, the other home base for Rounders, a hurling 'sliotar' is used (see p100), which has a cork core and a white pigskin outer.

The first formalised rules for Rounders were drawn up by the Gaelic Athletic Association in 1884, followed shortly afterwards by England's National Rounders Association, and whilst there are differences, the games are so similar that teams from both codes can and do readily compete against each other. A small number of other countries also play the game, although the 2008 world championships in Rotherham drew only four nations – England, Wales, China and Iran . . . who, unbelievably, won!

A Real Tennis court; favourite playground of Henry VIII.

SEPAK TAKRAW

You may never have heard of it, but in South East Asia this is *the* ball game. It involves a rather attractive-looking rattan ball and is not unlike volleyball, but without using your hands. Feet, knees, chest and head are the main parts of the body that come into play in this three-a-side game, so if you're good at keepy-uppy and gymnastics you've got a head start. (see picture on p180)

The game dates back at least 600 years in Thailand and Malaysia, although there were variations on both the name and the play in different south east Asian countries until 1866, when the Siam Takraw Association drew up the first set of rules for the sport. Now the world championships are held annually in Thailand.

Takraw balls were originally made out of a single woven layer of rattan, and this is still a popular material, although synthetic balls are also now used. Traditional style balls have a spherical shape and 12 holes with 20 intersections between the layers. Synthetic balls with softer synthetic coverings have recently been developed to lessen the impact on the player's body – foot volleys can reach in excess of 100kmph.

Dimensions are as follows: Circumference: 42cm (1ft 4½ins) to 44cm (1ft 5¼ins) for men and 43cm (1ft 5ins) to 45cm (1ft 5¾ins) for women; weight from 170g (6oz) to 180g (6.3oz) for men and from 150g (5.3oz) to 160g (5.6oz) for women.

ON THE BALL
"If you see a bicycle kick in soccer, it's a really rare occasion and everybody's applauding, but in Sepak Takraw you see it almost in every volley."
Daniel Angerhausen, secretary-general of the German Sepak Takraw Association
(Germany are Europe's strongest Sepak Takraw team).

STOOLBALL

To provide geographical balance for the inclusion of the thoroughly northern game of Knur and Spell, we have Stoolball, familiar to denizens of south east England, where it's played at local league level. It remains largely unknown outside that area.

The game originated in the 14th century in Sussex and was traditionally popular with milkmaids who used their milking stools as wickets. The ball is bowled full toss underarm from one end to the batter at the other – the links with cricket being obvious. The ball used in Stoolball is solid with a leather cover, much like a cricket ball, and there are other close similarities: each team has 11 players, the scoring system is very similar and a Stoolball game is also divided into overs, although of eight balls rather than six. Most modern stoolball teams are women only or mixed.

An alternative 'stoolball' was played by allied POWs in Colditz concentration camp during WWII, although this had nothing in common with 'real' Stoolball and appeared to consist primarily of an unruly scrum of chaps hurling themselves at another chap, who was perched on a stool, with the intention of sending him flying. This was not quite the piece of cake it sounds since there was a second scrum of chaps defending said chap on the stool. And there wasn't even a ball involved. Preposterous!

TCHOUKBALL

Tchoukball (pronounced 'chukeball') is not just a bit of a dog's dinner of a name it's also something of a dog's dinner of a game, comprising elements of handball, volleyball and squash. Two teams of nine players each attempt to score points by bouncing a ball onto either of two small angled trampolines at either end of a 16x32m court (you can score at both ends). After bouncing off the trampoline the ball must land outside a semi-circle facing said trampoline to score the point, but defenders are allowed to try to prevent it landing. There's a bit more to it than that, but those are the basic rules for what is actually a fast, fun sport that has taken off worldwide since being invented by Swiss biologist Dr. Hermann Brandt in the early 1970s. There are regular European and World championships – and Britain is actually reasonably good at Tchoukball, which makes a nice change.

The ball looks somewhat like a handball, with a leather covering and rubber bladder and diamond panelling. The circumference for men's balls should be 58-60cm and the weight 425-475g, and for women's and junior games it should be 54-56cm and 325-400g – the smaller ball is used in mixed games.

Tchoukball was invented as a non-violent sport, with the specific aim of avoiding contact injuries, that provides great exercise for both men and women, which shows just how 21st century it is – imagine getting a ninnyish idea like that past the inventors of traditional old sports like rugby . . .

CURVE BALL
Tchoukball is apparently named after the sound the ball makes as it bounces off the trampoline net. Oh, and there's a beach version of the game too – naturally.

TORBALL

Here's a nice one, because it shows just how inclusive sport can be when people make a bit of effort. Torball is a sport for the blind and visually impaired which uses a ball similar in size, shape and weight to a football, but with bells inside so its movements can be heard rather than seen.

It's played by two teams of three on opposite sides of a seven-metre wide indoor playing field in the middle part of which are three cords stretched across the entire width. At each end of the playing field is a goal that also stretches the entire width.

The idea is to score as many goals as possible by rolling the ball under the three cords into the goal of the opposing team. If the ball touches one of the cords, a penalty is called, where one player leaves the field and the remaining two players must try and defend their goal for one 'throw' by the opposing team.

WATER POLO

Yet another British gift to the world of sport (and at which, as usual, we're crap), Water Polo's origins hark back to hazy summer days when straight-backed young gentlemen from the country's public schools would take to the rivers winding past their alma maters with rugby balls or footballs and toss them around with gay abandon (and the balls too . . .).

Leather footballs and rugger balls are hardly conducive to proper competitive Water Polo games however, since they soak up water, gain weight and become slippery when wet – but it's strange that these balls were used in the first place since earlier games of what was initially called 'water rugby' had involved a smaller ball with a 3-4 inch diameter, which was made from rubber and presumably more 'playable'. But that's nobs for you – why make something easy when you can just as readily make it difficult (take cricket . . .)?

At the 1912 Olympics, the first games in which Water Polo appeared, a standard soccer ball was used, and it took a go-ahead American (let's get in a few national stereotypes while there's still chance) called James R. Smith to literally get to grips with the problem by developing a ball with an inflatable cotton bladder and a rubber fabric cover for better grip. That came along in 1936, and he also had the good sense to colour it red so spectators could see it better.

The bladder was later changed to nylon for improved performance, and in 1948 the official colour for competition play became yellow. By 1956 Smith's water polo ball had become the official ball for the Olympics and international games.

'Gripability' and visibility are vital components of a good water polo ball, so they're designed to be gripable by one hand despite the relatively large size. Plain yellow remained the colour of choice until 2005 when the international controlling body of the game (FINA) permitted a coloured middle stripe (blue, green, pink, red or black) across the normal yellow ball.

Vital stats are: weight 400-450g (14-16oz); inflated to approximately 90kPa (13PSI) of pressure; circumference 70cms or 28ins for size 5 balls for use by men, and 65cms or 26.5ins for size 4 balls for use by women.

International Water Polo – far removed from public schoolboys larking around in the river.

ZORBING

To be honest the only reason that I've included Zorbing is because I fancied having a sport beginning with 'Z' to bring an end to all this tomfoolery. After all, it's debatable whether actually being part of the very fabric of the ball in question means you're taking part in a ball game or you actually *are* the ball game . . .

Zorb (aka 'sphere') is actually the trademarked name of a transparent plastic sphere into which a deranged human scurries before bouncing downhill, or in some cases across water. Most spheres hold just one 'rider', although some have the capacity for two or even three human hamsters.

Originating in Rotorua, New Zealand, a zorb is a double-hulled sphere, with one ball inside the other with a layer of air in between to act as a shock absorber for the rider. The inner and outer sphere are connected by scores of small ropes and there are one or two tunnel-like entrances. There may be straps inside the zorb to allow the rider to hang on for dear life, or he/she may simply be tossed around inside as they bounce downhill or propel themselves across a lake, crashing into other Zorbers in bone-shaking fashion.

Typical dimensions of a Zorb are about 3m (9.8ft) in diameter, with an inner sphere size of about 2m (6.6ft), leaving a 50–60 centimetre (20–24 ins) air cushion around the riders. The plastic is approximately 0.8mm (0.031in) thick. This is obviously far and away the biggest ball in the book – which is kind of nice to finish on. And yes, naturally, the sport makes for ab-zorbing viewing . . .

So, there you have it – all the world's balls kicked, batted, nudged and shoved into some sort of order. Almost.

Because whilst the 40 or so balls described here arguably make up the most popular spheres in world sport, there are a hell of a lot of other minority ball sports around. Try this lot for starters, some of which you've no doubt never heard of…

Ball Tapping; Canoe Polo; Carpetball; Downball; Eton Ball Game; Eton Fives; Footbag; Footballtennis; Four Square; Harrow Football; Indiaca; Juggling; Kick-to-kick; Lotball; The Mesoamerican Ballgame; Newcomb Ball; PaddleBall; Paintball; Podex; Racquetball; Rapid Ball; Rockit Ball; Skee Ball; Stickball; Streetball; Table Football; Tee Ball; Tetherball; Tennis Polo/Toccer; Ulama; Water Basketball; Wiffleball; Winchester Football; Wireball.

You'll no doubt have a ball . . .